My Travelling Family

by

Eleanor Green

The Story of the

Mitchell Family

edited by
Tommy Green
additional material by
Kevin Scrivens

New Era Publications
2004

Published by:
New Era Publications
P.O. Box 549
Tweedale
Telford
TF7 5WA

The majority of photographs used in this
publication are from the family collection of
Tommy Green, with additional photographs
provided by the New Era Archive.
Other photographs are credited where known in
the captions, any omissions are unintentional.

ISBN 0 9535097 4 5

Printed by RCS Plc
Randall Park Way
Retford DN22 7WF

New Era Publications

PREFACE

Towards the end of her active life my mother chose to record her childhood memories. Her health was deteriorating and she did not finish the project.

Some twenty years on I have plucked up enough courage to edit and finish her manuscript. I have felt uneasy doing this. I was however heartened when I had modified a sentence and later found another draft of mother's with a similar remark.

When I asked aunt Jane if she would "proof read" she replied, "I would not dare correct Eleanor's work". I know exactly how she felt.

I believe that mother's work is an interesting contribution to social and fairground history.

My family showed a lack of imagination in choosing names. There are far too many Williams, Janes etc. My grandmother Mitchell had chosen "radical" names for her daughters, but acquiesced to the wish of others. To assist the reader there are two family trees at the back of this book .

In common with many I did not ask mother enough about her family. Fortunately I have her written word to tell me all I now want to know.

Deceember 2002

I was unaware when I wrote the preface in December 2002 that my mother had written an earlier draft manuscript around 1951. She had passed it on for safekeeping.

For whatever reasons, possibly mother thought she had lost it, she started again, from scratch in the late seventies.

During a recent tidy up the original manuscript resurfaced. The best efforts have been made to weld the two together.

I am indebted to Kevin Scrivens of New Era Publications whose experience, enthusiasm and perseverance has ensured the completion of this book.

Any errors in grammar, spelling, or construction are mine alone.

TOMMY GREEN
November 2003.

Contents

INTRODUCTION

In 1906, the year I was born, Queen Victoria had been dead for five years and the Edwardian era was in its heyday. It was a year when the hansom cab flourished, when women were clad in long floor sweeping dresses. They were wasp-waisted. My own mother boasted a 17 inch waist before she was married. Bathing machines were to be seen on the beaches and bathing costumes covered the wearer from neck to knee. Mr. Bernard Shaw was 50 and shocking the British theatregoer. Mr. Winston Churchill at 33 was making his mark in the House of Commons. The wonderful 17,000 ton Dreadnought was launched that year, an answer to the Kaiser's call for German equality on the seas.

The cinema had made its first appearance, known as the Bioscope, while the portable Gramophone could be heard up and down the land.

It was a peaceful world in 1906, a world in which the middle class was beginning to be recognised and one in which the working man was beginning to make his voice heard. The women of Britain had not yet been given the vote but they were clamouring and even fighting for it.

In Lancashire especially, it was a world of slums too, of evil smelling slums where children ran barefoot and poverty was rife, where unemployment meant the Poor Relief and where the Workhouse was dreaded by the old as much as in the days of Dickens. There was no welfare then and the threat of a pauper's death and funeral. It was the age of pride and poverty. People who could saved for a rainy day.

ELEANOR GREEN

Eleanor Mitchell (later Green), Hanover, September 1930

Grandad William Mitchell

MITCHELLS

I was born on the 10th of January 1906, in a bedroom over my maternal grandmother's small corner shop, 68 Stott Street, Hulme, South Manchester. There was, I know, some anxiety, as my mother, the last of the litter was considered the weakling of the family.

There was some annoyance too, on my grandmother's account, as someone stole a side of bacon out of the shop (which sold groceries and sweets). The loss was only noticed when it was too late to do anything but guess as to the culprit.

My grandmother Henshaw was an energetic, outspoken Lancashire woman of Irish parentage, and I can imagine that her remarks did justice to the occasion.

Because my father was a travelling showman our home was a caravan. The Mitchells had five caravans: grandfather's, one to each of his three sons and one for his only daughter. My parents' caravan was comfortable and well made. The inside had polished mahogany wood panels and the locker seats were upholstered in leather. There were

fifteen mirrors that shone and in which the brightly globed oil lamps twinkled and reflected my world. These mirrors made the living room seem larger than it really was. The floor was carpeted and kind to little feet. The lamps were supported by twisted silver holders and brackets. They had silver reflectors which prevented smoke from blackening the brightly painted ceiling. On the sideboard stood a silver stand with three silver dishes. Silver framed photographs twinkled from the mantelpiece. All these items were cleaned and polished every day.

The windows were cut glass and the table could accommodate four comfortably when the top was folded out. The fireplace contained a stove, a thing of beauty to my eyes, with its chrome plated door and fittings. There was a brass coal box which lay snugly underneath its shining fireguard and rails. A safety rail fitted on the top prevented pans from falling off. The oven would take a joint, usually a leg of lamb on Sunday, with roast potatoes and Yorkshire pudding. Carrots, peas and turnips would cook on the top inside the safety rail. There would

Grandfather Mitchell's Sea-on-Land ride and Tube Shooting Gallery at Colne in the 1890's. The family travelled two of these Savage built rides before the turn of the century, both with McLaren traction centre engines. The Tube Shooter is built onto the side of a living wagon, the two firing tubes actually passing through the wagon.

also be a large copper kettle on the stove, so that hot water was readily available. My parents were never poor nor were they ever wealthy, but Good Friday meant fresh salmon and new peas, Easter Sunday a spring chicken with new potatoes, Christmas Day turkey, plum pudding and mince pies and New Year's Eve a large pork pie and an iced cake to follow, all eaten after a bottle of port.

Mother took great pride in keeping everything shipshape and when she sang, which she frequently did, "I wouldn't leave my little wooden hut for you," we all knew she wouldn't. She was the well loved heart of my family.

The panels in the bedroom were painted with scenes of fruit and flowers. There were two big beds arranged in bunk bed fashion as in ships. Father, mother and the baby slept in the top bed and we three girls in the bottom one. We were snug and happy and this was home indeed. This was heaven and the great outside world meant as little to us as it did to newborn chicks under their mother's wing. Billy, three years older than me, slept with our cousins Billy and Benny in grandfather's caravan.

The fairground was our home and our playground and was accepted as naturally by us as fields by young lambs. When the fair was open, the lights lit and the organs playing, then we were in our element enjoying the rides and visiting the shows.

Grandad Mitchell had a total of fourteen grandchildren so there were plenty of companions. Uncle Willie's two children were however much older than we were. Jack, the older, was a great favourite with everyone. He had a ready smile and a merry way with him. He had only to enter a room for laughter to follow. As a young boy he with his mother at a Sunday school party. Various children had sung or recited, each one as prim and proper as the organisers could have wished for. Jack too wished for the limelight and continuously pressed his mother to allow him to go on the stage. One of the committee, hearing the small child, (golden haired, blue eyed and as angelic looking as a Reynold cherub), thought this a good idea and Jack accordingly took his stand to recite with great gusto:-

Paddy went-a walking one fine day,
Lost his trousers on the way,
How the women did laugh and the men did stare,
To see poor Paddy with his backside bare.

He was a great success.

Janie, his sister, was quiet and sedate and I saw little of her during my childhood.

It was a full and interesting life to us children, but we were not allowed to run wild. Meals were at regular hours and were good and wholesome. My mother insisted on our getting ready for bed around eight o'clock, when the dirt of the day had to be well washed off.

In bed, we could still hear the organs on each of the big rides. Each one played a different tune so it was a real medley. I can recall, "Roaming in the Gloaming," "She's a Lassie from Lancashire", "I know a Happy Little Girl", and the occasional dong of a wooden ball as it missed its target and hit the metal plate at the back of the coconut shy. The shouts of the crowds and the hammer hitting the bell on the "striker" which meant someone had won a prize. If there was a circus or a big show, you would hear the banging of a drum or the ringing of bells. I can recall at Wigan Fair watching from the bedroom the goings on at the front of the Boxing Show.

We could see the reflection of the lights of the Jumpers and the Cocks going round and round on the ceiling. We could hear the laughter of the crowds as they enjoyed the pleasures of the fair. But snug in our beds sleep invariably claimed us before the fair closed down at eleven o'clock or midnight. At Bolton New Year Fair the fair stayed open later to let in the New Year.

No matter how late the fair was open on Saturday night my father was always up and ready for church on Sunday morning. As soon as we were old enough we children went with him. My mother was a Protestant and did not go with us. I remember my cousin remarking how very convenient this was as the Sunday dinner of those days needed every attention and we were always ready for it when we returned.

A strange peace would pervade the fairground on a Sunday. In these colliery towns no matter how unruly the neighbours had been during the week, on a Sunday you could almost have heard a pin drop. The children clad in their Sunday best would be quiet and well behaved.

Woe betide any child who returned home with his clothes the worse for wear. Families were large, wages low, and clothes expensive. Children knew that "Sunday Best" was "Sunday Best" and had to last the expected time.

Mother and our Living Van

On Monday, irksome restraint was forgotten and the busy life took shape again. How I loved riding on the jumpers, uncle Bennie's wooden galloping horses, and also the cocks, which my father at one time owned. They were jerky in movement and as the cockerels head pitched forward so would mine and I found it rather frightening.

Our big boats too, "Shamrock" and "Defender", needed all one's attention and balance. Janie was sick every time she went aboard while I swayed from right to left, as I saw our workers do, and kept my feet without holding on to the rail. I always had the fear that I might fall and finish the ride ignominiously.

With the jumpers I had no such fear, up and down went the horses, gliding round in their perpetual circle. I had seen Ada Proctor who rode horseback in the circus. How I envied her, standing up, turning round, jumping to the ground and leaping back a few seconds later. I knew there was no hope of my doing anything like that so I would do my best to imitate her on my wooden steed, facing the tail, then turning while the ride was still going and facing the head. I would then stand on the horse with one leg outstretched, but both my hands holding the brass pole. However, I had to be careful, as my uncle Willie would let my parents know if he saw me. My cousin Lucy sometimes joined in the fun, but if her brothers saw us they would put a stop to our capers. I remember Bennie saying, "If there was a tribe of Red Indians on the ground, our Lucy would join them and have feathers in her hair."

At one time my father bought a Joy Wheel, built by Orton & Spooner. How I loved this ride. I would rush to the centre and glue my hands down flat to the "wheel" and usually managed to stay the distance. On the outer edge of the wheel, one of our workmen was dressed in a white sweater and blue trousers. He would dance to the delight of the audience. The Joy Wheel was not a financial success and my father sold it after a short run.

Another ride of the times was a Razzle Dazzle. This was a drum shaped roundabout mounted on a short tower which swayed from side to side as it went round. This was also a great favourite with us.

"Pulling down day" was always exciting. My father would be up at an early hour. While my mother busied herself with the breakfast, we children would kneel on the top bed and look out of the vents of the mollycroft, and watch the progress. The big traction engines (each with its own name proudly displayed in brass) would be chugging backwards and forwards across the ground. Trucks would be loaded and those in awkward positions would be levered out with long ski like wooden

Wallis's four abreast Jumpers at Bootle. This ride was later owned by Uncle Bennie Mitchell. To the left is a travelling cinema show, and to the right a set of Steam Yachts owned by Isaac Richards.

10

Uncle Bennie's Platform Cocks ride at Rochdale. This ride was at one time travelled by my Father Thomas Mitchell.

Father's Steam Yacht ride and Grandad's Platform Cockerels at Burnley Fair 1906. The ride in the background is Mrs Holden's Platform Cocks and Horses.

The Joy Wheel at Hull Fair. This was a combination of a ride and a show. Members of the audience were invited to sit on the wooden spinning disc at the centre and see if they could remain on the wheel as it increased in speed. Invariably everyone was spun off into the cushioned barriers. Members of staff became adept at walking and even dancing on the moving wheel.

Edmund Holland's steam driven Razzle Dazzle. The fair organ on the front carries the makers inscription 'Peter Varetto, Oldham Road, Manchester'.

Steam traction engine "Lancashire Lad", number 12940 built by Fosters of Lincoln, was new to Grandad in 1912 for haulage and generating electricity for the new Scenic Railway ride. The illustration was used in advertising by the manufacturers.

iron-shod levers. They would then be coupled together usually in threes, and hitched up behind the appropriate traction engine.

We particularly liked to watch the cocks, a roundabout not unlike the jumping horses. When the cocks were ready for the road that was a sight indeed. The traction engine would steam majestically out followed by as many as nine two wheeled trucks, zigzagging like a crazy snake to the next destination. How the tram drivers hated them! Once the procession reached the main road, if a tram happened to be travelling in the same direction, it was goodbye to all hopes of keeping to its timetable. Clang on the bell as he may, he was a lucky driver who could overtake the cocks. Luckily we usually travelled short distances, in many instances the fairs being only two or three miles apart.

The Lancashire roads were mostly made of stone blocks or setts, 6 inches square. Most of the wheels of our various vehicles were of wood bound with iron bands. This was before the popularity of rubber tyres and as a consequence every journey was a slow one. The caravan would rattle and creak as it moved along the road.

Prior to moving to the next fair every article of glass and china had to be packed around with cloths to prevent it becoming cracked or broken. The cut glass paraffin lamps and holders too had to be packed away and the most precious ornament, a camel made by Royal Dux, would be laid in the bed and packed around with pillows. This camel was about fourteen inches high, it was mother's pride and joy and an object of beauty to all of us. This was the first item to be packed away and the first to be unpacked on arrival at our next fairground.

The traction engine was the heart of the roundabout, supplying power when on the fairground, and on the road hauling the loads from one site to another. There was no need for billposting in those days. Our family had five traction engines, each one as distinctive and as temperamental as a prima donna. When these traction engines were on route, the noise could be heard for at least a mile. Sometimes sacks had to be put under the wheels of the traction engine to make them grip when ascending a hill. Occasionally a horse would pull our caravan, and as we usually travelled in it mother would get us to walk up any steep hills to make the load lighter. As we approached the outskirts of the town we were going to, the noise of the traction engine which was ahead of us would attract the local children who would run to us shouting, "the Wakes, the Wakes." When we arrived on the fairground more children were there to welcome us and watch the various caravans being put into place. The rides were erected next and the stalls etc. later. We were always welcome when we entered a town and the many people we knew were always sorry to see us go.

We generally travelled South Lancashire, visiting the colliery towns. My grandfather had done this for at least 50 years before I was born and he was as well known as many of the local people.

We children loved to ride on the traction engine and occasionally my father would let us do so. Round the fairground he would go with Billy, Janie, May and I all sitting in the coal box. "Shall I Do It" was the nickname of this engine. It was a huge one and while it did not have any of the glamour of "Lancashire Lass", "Lancashire Lad" or "Her Majesty", (my uncles' engines) it had plenty

of character and was well loved by us.

When my brother Tom began to sit up and take notice it was "Shall I Do It" which became his first interest. His arms would flay the air like a miniature flywheel and he was adept in making the individual noises of the engine before he was two. Our Great Dane, Duchess, could hear our engine long before we could, and would leap into the air to announce its arrival.

When Tom left college he joined the Customs and Excise. During the war he volunteered and joined Bomber Command. He became a navigator on a Wellington bomber and then a Halifax. His plane was shot down over Holland on the night of 22nd June 1943 and he was the only survivor. He became a P.O.W. and was at Stalag Luft VI in Poland for a while. At the end of the war he was repatriated, and after considerable medical attention, he returned to his old job. In time he became a "surveyor". He died in 1978 age 63.

Fathers traction engine known as "Shall I Do It". It was one of several traction engines owned by Mitchells which were built by McLarens of Leeds. Some of these engines were built into the centre of the rides to drive them round. To the left are cousin Lucy, Herbert Portlock (with bowler hat and watch chain), who was a manager for Mitchells, Mother with the dog, and cousin Benny with crutches. The steel back wheels of the engine have been fitted with wooden blocks to help prevent skidding on the cobbled highways of Lancashire.

GRANDAD

My grandfather, the head of the firm, was the organiser or lessee of many Lancashire fairgrounds, including Rochdale, Accrington, Radcliffe, Atherton and Leigh. Grandad's father was also called William and his wife Elizabeth was a Whittam before her marriage. They lived in Sharpe St. Manchester. Great grandfather was registered as a baker, and this probably referred to the fact that he made gingerbread and brandy snap to sell on the fairground. This is borne out by the first printed letter headings, which had the caption, "Founded when George the Fourth was King". This King died in 1830 so great grandfather must have founded the firm as grandad was born in 1840. Great grandad died when only a young man in 1853. His widow now had two children to bring up, William and Elizabeth. William was a go-getter but the family had very little money. He worked hard and long from a tender age delivering bags of coal in a little home-made truck, doing any job that came to hand, seeking work and invariably finding it.

Drudging, trudging his young life away until in his early twenties he concentrated on the Lancashire markets and fairs in and around Bolton. He made and sold toffee on them. He had two big dogs, (Dutch barge hounds, I believe) which pulled his cart. With these he went to Bolton, Bury, Heywood, Rochdale and other Lancashire towns and villages. In time he was able to buy a pony, which could pull a larger cart which enabled him to go further afield. He saved every penny he could and then bought his first small roundabout. This was hand operated. That "made money" so he bought a larger one. Before many years had passed he had four large roundabouts and five traction engines. With traction engines driving dynamos the rides could all be lit by electricity. When his fair visited some villages it was the first time some of the residents had seen electric light. This sensation caused them to come onto the fair and subsequently spend money. He used to advertise well in advance, "This Fair will be illuminated by electricity, regardless of cost".

Grandad regularly changed his roundabouts, often buying from manufacturers Savages of King's Lynn. Amongst the rides he owned were two sets of Mountain Ponies, two Sea on Land rides, three sets of Cocks, and a Razzle Dazzle.

He had also visited Europe. These business trips were for the inspection and purchase of mechanical organs for use on his roundabouts. At least one of the organs was bought from the firm of Gavioli who were based in Paris.

He was a great believer in education and, when still very young (in his teens I believe), he paid thrupence a week for schooling. He regularly banked money and if doing so asked the state of his account(s). When he acquired roundabouts or traction engines, he paid for these through his bank account. Always reluctant to part with cash he would pay by cheque quite willingly. He kept his cash in a safe in his living wagon. When we went back to boarding school, he always gave us a silver thrupenny bit, while other relations thought half a crown more suitable. Saving, buying, saving, buying, eventually he became a man of property.

Grandad Mitchell in typical attire with his clogs and the thick gold watch chain which he always wore.

15

Grandad's steam driven Motor Car ride at Newchurch in Rossendale 1905. The novelty of motor cars on roundabouts had only been introduced that year, and Mitchells' was one of the first rides to be fitted with them.

He owned houses in Skiddaw Street, Blackburn, and at least twenty nine in Heywood. He bought Angel Meadow fairground also in Heywood.

Meanwhile he married my grandmother Jane who bore him four children. She died when my father was nine and whilst still in her thirties. My grandfather later married her widowed sister, who had two children, James and Margaret Fearns. This second wife, Eleanor, was kindness herself to the family. She died before I was born but my father named me after her as a token of his affection.

Each of grandad's three sons had a roundabout. The other tenants at his fairs were mostly stallholders (having hooplas, emmas and coconut shies/sheets). The majority of these showmen were either relations of Mitchells or my mother. It was like a travelling village with my grandfather in the role of Lord of the Manor. His word was law and while he may not have been beloved he was certainly respected.

Uncle Willie, his eldest son had a motor car Scenic Railway roundabout. Uncle Bennie, the second son, had an adult set of jumping horses, and the Cocks. My father (Thomas), the youngest son, had a set of steam yachts. Aunt Lucy, the only daughter and youngest child, had married showman

Henry Jennings. They later had the set of Cocks, which were replaced in the 1920's by a set of adult Chairoplanes. Grandfather lived for his sons, and his grandsons were participants and possible future controllers of the business. He was a conscientious Roman Catholic and all his children attended good Catholic schools.

His approach to public relations was, "Tell 'em nowt". If annoyed he would exclaim, "Damn, bugger and blast." He smoked a pipe, enjoyed a glass of rum and was good, witty and interesting company. In 1889 he was a one of the founders and pioneer members of The Van Dwellers association (later renamed The Showmen's Guild). William was a member of the earliest recorded Committee of 1892, continuing this interest throughout his life. He was a regular member of the Committee and both he and his son Bennie were members of the 1907 Committee of the Showmen's Guild.

Grandad Mitchell wore distinctive clothes for a showman. His hat was a cross between a top hat and a bowler, fawn in colour and with a slightly upturned brim. His coat was of the "cut away" type with tails, and his trousers were narrow as drainpipes. He wore stiff two inch winged collars and a broad silk tie.

16

Grandfather however was no dandy and very often this costume was worn above a pair of Lancashire clogs which he found comfortable and weatherproof. He was a strong man. He was knocked down and run over by a van when in his seventies and his leg was badly hurt, or so we thought. Mother bathed it twice a day with some herbal mixture he asked her to get. In a matter of weeks he was back to normal without signs of a limp.

He had a good appetite and enjoyed stews of all description: oxtail soup, with the bone left in of course, sheep's head broth, tripe and onions, steak and cow heel, steak and kidney (with dumplings) and neck and broth with barley. He rarely ate biscuits or cakes, but made toffee or nougat for the family. We children loved watching him make it and we ate it while it was still warm. He also made brandy snap, rolling it out in curls. There was never any left; it was eaten as it was made and he enjoyed it as much as we did.

Grandfather Mitchell lived in his own caravan though mother cooked his meals and he ate with us. My younger sister May, born in 1910, was a fussy little girl, who would take her time eating and only enjoyed sweet food. Grandad was watching her one day and, just as she raised her spoon to her mouth, he pushed it away. She didn't say a word, but when he did it a second time she emptied the plate of food over his head, his beard getting soaked too. Mother was upset but grandfather wouldn't hear of May being smacked. "She did quite right," he said, "I shouldn't have teased her. Don't punish her. I like a child with spirit." But mother took care that May did not sit near grandfather again.

His sight was poor due to cataracts. In those days nothing could be done to remedy or improve his vision.

There were two double bunk beds in his caravan. He slept in the top one, and three of his teenage grandsons slept in the bottom one. The boys said that he always said goodnight to the portrait of his first wife Jane before he went to bed. They thought this a great joke. Grandad had a magnificent gold pocket watch, which showed the phases of the moon and had a tinkling bell which chimed. We all liked to hold and listen to it. I think this was a Thomas Russell of Liverpool. It was a keyless full hunter (a watch with a lid to protect the face and watchglass) and it seemed to be larger in diameter than the usual watch.

These watches were always worn with a

Mitchells' Scenic Motor Cars, 4-abreast Galloping Horses, and Steam Yachts at St. Helens. The May Pole in the foreground is probably related to an event organised by St. Christopher's Roman Catholic Church.

medallion called an "Albert". The watch chain had a swivel bar or "T" bar in the centre of the chain which slotted into the buttonholes of the waistcoat. The other end of the chain usually carried a gold or silver matchbox. Some showmen had the waistcoat pocket lined with wash leather to prevent the watch surface being scratched. Grandad's thick gold watch chain also had a gold lion on it, dangling half way down the chain. Our boys, my brothers and cousins, used to take great delight in announcing that grandad had been feeding the lion again, a reference to him spilling some soup or broth when he was eating. This family joke was never said nastily and always out of grandad's hearing. But he was no joke. He held the reins of the business firmly in his strong aged hands, and his active brain and wonderful memory won our respect.

We all respected grandad except the two youngest grandchildren, my sister May and Tom, the baby of the family. Grandad taught Tom to play cards, usually "Snap", and after about five minutes play we would hear Tom shouting, "you are cheating grandad. mammy, grandad is cheating again, I am not playing with him anymore". He would run out in high dudgeon, we could hear grandad chuckling and about ten minutes later Tom would be back playing cards. Grandad's sight was so poor that he had to have all his correspondence read out to him, usually by one of his grandchildren. One day my cousin Benny, then about fifteen, read him a letter asking for a position at one of his fairs for a show exhibiting two "bare" ladies. Grandad could not believe that anyone would think he would allow the showing of bare ladies on one of his fairgrounds, he prided himself on catering for families. However he felt that something was wrong. He got Benny to bring a trusted older showman into his caravan and asked Benny to read the letter again.

Grandad explained his astonishment, "If I accommodated them no Corporation would trust me again, what do you make of it?" The showman said he would make enquiries, which he did, and the mystery was solved. "It's not bare ladies Mr. Mitchell, they are billed as "bear" ladies, and I believe they are very good and perfectly respectable too. They prefer to walk on all fours, are dark skinned and have no elbows. They also speak several languages and have been on one or two fairgrounds in this country already, with no complaints." In view of this grandad accepted the

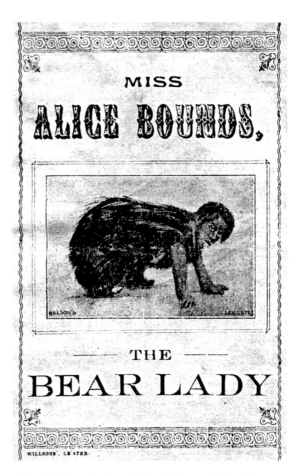

MISS
ALICE BOUNDS,

THE
BEAR LADY

WILLSONS. LE'STER.

A handbill for the Bear Lady which caused Grandad some consternation.

booking and "The Bear Ladies" appeared a few weeks later. I saw them and was fascinated by their appearance and their way of saying "Goodnight" to the onlookers in different languages.

Grandad only allowed one lady to appear on his grounds with a "tick off", a character reading much favoured by teenage girls. However, a person billing herself as a genuine fortune teller asked if she could put her tent up on one of his fairgrounds and grandad gave way to her pressure. Unfortunately when it came to paying her rent, which was only a few shillings she asked to be excused. She explained that as it had rained every day she had taken very little money. Grandad would not agree to this at all, "You are the fortune teller, not me, and you were very anxious to come. In view of this, I thought we were on to a good thing. I am more disappointed than you and my expenses are greater."

Another time when a traveller with a sweet stall

complained of terrible business and that the rent was too dear, William said very little in reply, but asked if he had any empty nougat boxes to spare. Anxious to please the lessee, the tenant brought him a good supply. William then enquired how he could empty so many boxes if business was so poor.

Uncle Bennie died on 12th July 1918. My father passed away less than twelve months later. Despite this double tragedy grandad carried on, presiding over the decline of what had been the most successful fairground firm in Lancashire.

William attended the 1922 Preston Guild Fair, (a two week event, particular to Preston, and held every twenty years). He had been present at five "Guilds", 1842, 1862, 1882, 1902 and 1922. At the 1922 event business was bad and William, then age 82, said he would not bring his roundabouts to the next Guild, which was due to be held in 1942.

William outlived all his contemporaries and was the "Grand Old Man" or "Father of Travelling Showmen". He was sometimes called, "Old Blower" which originates from "Puffing Billy". He was also known as "Bolton Billy" or "Grandad Mitchell" and he walked with a stick latterly. Although William owned so much property he always lived in his modest showman's living wagon.

He died on 28th April 1928 at Atherton and was interred in the family vault at Preston. His estate was valued at £15,479.2s.9d. a significant achievement considering he started from next to nothing. He left the bulk of his estate to his surviving son William.

To his daughter Lucy Hannah Jennings he left a roundabout and thirteen houses in Railway St. and Green Lane, Heywood. To my mother, in trust for her children, eleven houses in Gregge St. and five houses in Robert St. Heywood. There were other bequests to members of the family.

One of the motor cars on Grandad's Steam Switchback. The cars had rubber tyres and were upholstered in leather. In 1905 it was considered quite something to be able to ride in a motor car. The BN registration on one of the cars was a Bolton number, the other registrations would also have been local to the area the ride travelled in. Behind the motor car is one of the mechanical organs which Grandad went specially to Paris to buy from the firm of Gavioli.

FATHER

My Father, Thomas, and Mother, Rachael.

My father Thomas Mitchell was the youngest son and was born in Ramsbottom in 1877. He was educated at St. Ignatius School, Preston, and then at the Catholic College, Preston, though it was then called The Christian Brothers School.

He was cautious with money. Though of average height he was bull necked. He was a teetotaller and, unlike his brothers, did not gamble. He was not as robust as his father and was a finicky eater. A slave to work, but a loving family man. He enjoyed having his five children round him, asking us questions like "Which is the longest river in England?" or "Which is the biggest county in England?" We all shared the prize, bars of milk chocolate.

We were usually on the Lancashire fairgrounds, but occasionally we went further afield. My father once took a roundabout to Hull Fair.

He was a good husband and provider which is evidenced by sending a son and three daughters to boarding school. As a young man father was reputed to have ridden a motor bike down the one

hundred and twenty two stone steps that led from St Chad's Church, Rochdale. I can recall his anger when a bag of "takings" was dropped and the cash spilled everywhere whilst on their way from the Yachts ride to the living wagon. I can also remember, when we visited a picture hall, his tears when the lights came on at the end of a sad film. When a female member of the family said mother was making a fuss about having a baby, he replied, "She is not a cart horse like you." Like his father and brothers he could be witty. I was told that when mother's first baby Billy was christened my father made a toast: "May he be as lucky as his grandfather, as witty as his grandmother, as loving as his mother and as handsome as his dad."

My father drove our traction engine, "Shall I Do It". It was the oldest, noisiest and least attractive traction engine Mitchells had. Nevertheless he could coax it into doing its job. It was hard, hot and dirty work driving a traction engine. It was also a bumpy and jolting task driving the engine on cobbles. There was no cab or roof to protect father

The Joy Wheel ride that Father took to Hull Fair. It must have been new when it was photographed as it is undecorated apart from paper posters.

The same ride some time later when it had been professionally decorated and fitted with an entrance surrounded by carved woodwork.

Oldham Wakes Fair 1905. The fair was held on ground known as Tommyfield, which was actually a cobbled market place. To the left are Father's Steam Yachts next to John Collins' four abreast Gallopers.

and his assistant in inclement weather.

During the Great War father was conscripted to work in a Sheffield steelworks. The harsh conditions and working indoors seriously affected his health. After the war father returned to run his steam yachts. Dad contracted cancer and the last days of his life were spent at Maines Farm, Preston. Grandad arranged with business rival, John Green, for him to be nursed at John's son-in-law's farm. He died there on 11th June 1919 aged 42.

My mother became a tower of strength and did her best to make up for my father's absence. He had denied himself many little luxuries in the hope that he was building for the future, and my mother became determined that we should not be cheated. For several months she indulged in a spending spree. A Foden showman's engine to replace the McLaren "Shall I Do It", (she partly blamed this old engine for my fathers death), a new caravan to replace the old one which she gave to one of father's cousins, and a new diamond mourning ring for herself. She continued travelling the Steam Yachts until 1925 when they were sold to Greens of Preston.

Following Father's death in 1919 Mother bought Foden traction engine number 2106, named "Dreadnought" to replace the old McLaren "Shall I Do It". The Foden was new in 1910 to Simons and Greatorex and had worked with their Galloping Horse ride. When Mother sold the Yachts in 1925 the engine was sold to Henry O'Brien in Scotland.

UNCLE WILLIE MITCHELL

William or uncle Willie was the eldest son and his father's favourite. He was born in Preston in 1869 and was educated at Roper's School, 39 Back Lane, Preston. As an adult, he always operated the family's best roundabout.

William Jnr. married Emma MacIndoe, sister of John Green's wife. They had four children, two of whom lived to become adults, John William (known as Jack) and Janie (Tom and another infant died as a result of illness). In 1911, Emma died and William later married Mary Dearden, who had been a friend of Emma's. Mary was born in the Orkney Islands. She was very kind and well liked. She died in 1937, aged sixty seven.

After his father's death in 1928 William inherited the travelling business and the bulk of his dad's estate which made him a wealthy man. He continued to run the business, with son Jack being in day to day charge.

Willie liked to gamble and enjoyed a pint. He was good company in the pub. He spent hours studying a dictionary and was well practised in trick questions. When asked when Mossley Wakes Fair was held, he would reply, "On the third Saturday after the second fall of snow." In an era when showmen sent fairground trucks by rail and were charged according to the weight, William prided himself on giving an incorrect one. He boasted that he never robbed a man of a day's work, and his children were his own work and without the help of a lodger. His third wife, Linda, was at one time landlady of the Brunswick Hotel, Heywood.

William bought a semi-detached house, "Lisborne", 196 Devonshire Road, Blackpool and they lived there in semi-retirement until his death on 5th October 1946, age 77.

Jack in turn became the custodian of the business which he ran successfully. He passed the baton to his cousin Billy (son of my uncle Bennie) shortly before his death in 1966.

In 1912 Grandad and the family invested a huge amount of money in the very latest technology of the time, an electrically propelled Scenic Motor Car ride. Uncle Willie was in charge of this machine. It was featured on the front page of the Worlds Fair showmen's newspaper when it was new, with Fathers Yachts to the left and the Joy Wheel to the right.

Uncle Willie's Motor Car Scenic building up at St.Helens. This shows the huge amount of scenery in the centre of the ride. The engine "Lancashire Lad" has pulled the car truck under a build up crane gantry to transfer the heavy Motor Cars onto the track of the ride. Using traction engines for haulage enabled much larger trucks like the one on the right to be used, instead of the smaller horse drawn vehicles, several of which can be seen in the photograph.

The Scenic Railway at the same location with the deep foliage rounding boards fitted and made ready for opening. The traction engine has been positioned at the side of the ride to generate electricity, and fitted with a tall extension chimney to carry the smoke away from the attractions.

UNCLE BENNIE (BENJAMIN) MITCHELL

Uncle Bennie's Platform Cocks ride, which was a mixture of cockerels and ostriches. Each of the step boxes under the birds carried a slogan, the one in view reads 'He who envies admits his inferiority'. The ride in the background is Uncle Willie's Scenic Motors, and the location is Rochdale. The sign top right reads "Old Firm" and is attached to Butterworth's Pea Saloon.

Second son Bennie was born in Blackburn in 1872. His father was anxious for his children to be educated and, as soon as he could afford it, he sent Bennie to boarding school. However, Bennie hated it and ran away, coming back to the fairground and his father. Grandfather then sent him to another school but he was back within a month. It was then arranged for him to go to a Catholic College in Bruges, Belgium. Bennie stayed there (hating it) until he was fourteen. After he left school he helped his father on the fairground and found that much more to his liking.

As soon as he was old enough to manage a small roundabout, grandfather bought him a set of "Dobbies". I think this was a fairground corruption of "hobby horses". Later he had various adult roundabouts. His last ride was a four-a-breast set of gallopers.

Uncle Bennie was a "caution." He had a tremendous, almost childlike, sense of fun and also

on occasion a sadistic sense of humour. He was five years older than my father. When he was in his late twenties he married Lizzie the daughter of Colonel Clark. He owned and operated one of the earliest travelling "silent" cinemas. Bennie and Lizzie had seven children but only two boys and two girls survived infancy. Bennie loved his children and the favourite was his elder daughter Lizzie who was the apple of his eye. Our cousins were more like brothers and sisters to us and uncle Bennie being full of fun, was always our favourite uncle.

Lively, kindly, olive-skinned Rubenesque aunt Lizzie and her irrepressible husband, who was as full of pranks as a schoolboy. Nothing delighted him more than to dance on the roof of my grandmother Henshaw's caravan in the dead of night or to breathe on the window when it was dark and make harrowing, haunting noises with his forehead on the damp surface. Often when he knew my grandmother was in bed, and her daughters who normally cosseted her had gone out on some errand, he would enter the wagon, bid her dress and laughingly persuade her to visit the nearest pub where he would ply her with drink. Then he would bring her safely home, laughing gleefully at the rueful faces of my poor aunts. But uncle Bennie was well liked and so it was always taken in good part.

Uncle Bennie was a gambler who loved horses, horse racing, bowls and every place where men gathered to woo the goddess of chance. The prize meant nothing, but the winning everything. He was however, interested in his business. Bennie was as different as chalk and cheese to his thrifty and hard working father.

When uncle Bennie had had a drink or two he was inclined to argue and occasionally to boast. Then he was a Hercules, a lifter of weights, a runner of races, and a holder of jumping records. His traction engine was the best and the strongest in the North. His elder brother Willie was inclined to argue and boast too. When they met in the public house and the fire of battle had been well kindled by the spirits they had imbibed, challenges were flung. On one occasion they left the pub, heaped coal on the dampened fires of the traction engines, got steam up, and after marking out a boundary, chained "Lancashire Lass" to "Her Majesty" and started a tug of war between the two steel giants. An interested group of spectators spurred them on and bets were taken. Then my grandfather, almost frothing with wrath, bore down on them and stopped the contest.

On another occasion uncle Bennie and uncle Willie were wrangling as to who was the better

Uncle Bennie.

runner. Uncle Bennie was convinced he could beat uncle Willie not only on the flat but also with his brother running down hill and he running uphill. The race was arranged for the following night. They were both to start from two milestones and meet at the milestone in the centre, uncle Bennie's mile being uphill and uncle Willie's level. Uncle Bennie with several confederates arranged to move the centre milestone before the race. How they did this and how far it was moved I cannot say, but so many people have told me the story that I feel it is true. The milestone was moved for such a distance

Uncle Bennie's hand turned juvenile Dobby ride bought for him when he left school by Grandad.

The Elaborate travelling silent cinema, or Bioscope Show, which was travelled by Uncle Bennie's father in law Colonel Clark.

that uncle Bennie easily won his race, to his brother's surprise and discomfort. It was many years before uncle Willie learned the truth.

On another occasion, when horses were still being used, uncle Bennie's father-in-law had arrived at Rochdale fairground and parked his caravan in the usual position with the others. Uncle Bennie was feeling merry that evening and was having a drink in the public house with a friend who owned horses and was a carrier. Bennie asked him if he would move Colonel Clark's caravan that night to the Town Hall Square. His friend readily agreed. It was then dark, but his horses were near at hand and as uncle Bennie insisted on urgency, he promised to move it immediately. "But" said uncle Bennie, "father-in-law is a heavy drinker and it's quite possible he will object. Do not take any notice of him. He will be the first to thank you in the morning, as he is really anxious to be on the Town Hall Square." The two had by this time toasted each other in various glasses. Nothing would please his friend more than to carry out uncle Bennie's wishes. So off with his horse he went, hitched it to the shafts and away went caravan and horse with Bennie's companion on the footboard.

Colonel Clark, who was a sober and kindly widower, had retired for the night. The lamps were out, the caravan in darkness. Imagine his horror when, with a jolt that nearly shook him out of bed, he felt his home being moved along at some considerable speed. Rushing to the door he could just distinguish the driver and the horse which was hauling him onward. "Stop," he yelled, "What ever are you doing?" But the carter didn't turn a hair. "Go back to bed," he said virtuously. "You ought to be ashamed of yourself getting drunk at your age. Your son-in-law has told me all about you."

So in spite of Colonel Clark's protests, off to the Town Hall went the caravan with Colonel Clark inside. There it stayed until the following morning. Many good people of Rochdale still remember the day when they rubbed their eyes in amazement at the sight of Colonel Clark's caravan on their Town Hall Square.

Bennie was very well liked and had a devil may care attitude to problems. Wherever he went his dog Jack, a black and white terrier, went too and, as Bennie was a frequenter of the local pubs, the dog, waiting outside, gave the game away. Bennie was not a heavy drinker although he would gamble on anything.

He fell victim to the Spanish flu epidemic that killed more people than the Great War, and died as a result of it at Bolton in 1918, age 47.

AUNT LUCY MITCHELL/JENNINGS

Lucy Anne was grandad's only daughter. Her mother died when she was less than three years old, and she was then boarded with the Kelly family. She had great affection for them because of the love they had shown her. When she was of suitable age she was sent as a boarder to an excellent convent in Preston.

Grandfather would not tell lies and insisted on his children telling him the truth, no matter how unpleasant. Aunt Lucy told me that he said to her, "Tell the truth and shame the devil." She was very straightforward and truthful to a fault.

She married showman William Henry Jennings. They had two daughters and a son. Tragically young William Henry was killed in a road accident aged eight. Eldest daughter Elizabeth died as a result of a fire whilst in hospital waiting to give birth. She was married to Arthur Silcock and was only twenty three at the time of her death. Aunt Lucy was a hard worker and energetic. Despite the two tragedies in her life she made the best of things. After she and husband Henry sold their adult chairoplanes they operated juvenile rides. Following Henry's death she continued in business. Younger daughter Lucy Maria (Lulu) married Charles Hart and had two children. Lulu and her

Aunt Lucy.

husband eventually took over aunt Lucy's business. She died in 1966 age eighty two. Lulu died in 1999 aged 81.

Preston Whitsuntide Fair 1930. Uncle Henry Jennings' Chairoplanes to the right. The family's four abreast is riding well. Green's number two Caterpillar is on the right. My husband Bob and I ran this ride in the first year of our marriage, 1937. The headboard or proscenium of Green's Yachts (formerly Mitchell's) can be seen above the Chairoplanes.

Aunt Janie with one of the dogs, and Aunt Nellie in the doorway of their Living Wagon, which was built by Pollits of Bolton. It was cleverly designed to be low enough to pass under the loading gauges of the railways when sent on a rail carriage truck.

My first recollection is of being taken to visit my mother in 1910 while my brother Billy and I were staying at our great aunt's house in Salford. Mother had just had her fourth child in her mother's house at 10 Collinge Street, Heywood, a small Lancashire cotton town to which grandmother had moved two years previously after she had finished with the shop in Manchester. We were told by auntie that we had a new baby sister and that mother wanted us to go and see her. When we arrived there, we rushed upstairs to find mother sitting up in bed, smiling.

"The baby mammy, the baby, where is it?" "What baby?" asked mother and then, seeing our tragic faces, uncrooked her arm, lifted her shawl and we saw our baby sister for the first time. "Tell her to open her eyes," said Billy, then he kissed mother and rushed downstairs to tell my father all the news.

The baby was to be "May", born in the month of May, but the Registrar of Births recorded "Mary Ann" (after my grandmother) and the name was a source of sorrow to May and of ironic amusement to the rest of the family throughout her childhood. I think we must have gone to the christening, though I cannot remember anything of that day.

I was quite happy to stay with mother and the baby. The bedroom was very big, with a four poster bed and a bedhead of red velvet with gold embroidery about six feet above the mattress. On a table near the bed was a disc musical box which played popular songs. The record seemed to be made of thick cardboard with holes in it and the tunes were reedy but clear and we could all sing as it played.

My father took me down the stairs which seemed very steep, and I was glad to get into the living room. This was another big room. There was a piano in one corner of the room with green pleated silk under a kind of fretwork and with candlesticks, but these were never lit as grandma was nervous of fire. In the centre of the room was a huge mahogany table, about 6 feet in diameter with a central carved leg supporting it. On a small table in the opposite corner to the piano, was a glass case filled with stuffed birds, canaries and budgerigars which were perched on twigs. Alongside was a dish of artificial fruit: peaches, grapes, and bananas, all beautifully arranged. The two sets of lustres on the mantelpiecc moved and tinkled gently every time the door was opened. There was also a large clock on the wall. It chimed every quarter of an hour and was the type usually seen in schools.

The living room had a big fireplace, which would take a bucketful of coal easily, and this gave plenty of heat. My father had bought two Dutch plates, which he put up over the mantelpiece. A few years later he bought a magnificent painting of Christ being taken down from the Cross. He paid £15 for it in 1918 and we thought it must be worth a great deal of money. The two dogs were in and out, excited at seeing us, remembering us although we had been away. My grandmother busied herself with the baking of the bread, and with the dough pigs she made specially for Billy and myself, with

currants for eyes.

Auntie Nellie tended my mother upstairs taking her gruel or oyster soup, while auntie Janie bustled in and out of the room seeming perpetually busy. My father, his large brilliant dark eyes full of fun, spoke of "another little suffragette" in the family.

On the other side of Collinge Street were smaller houses with quite small rooms and very little furniture. We knew everyone who lived there. They were friendly people but very poor, as most folks were in the North at that time. The milkman came round every day with his horse and cart, ladling pints and half pints out, pouring whatever was required into the owner's jugs. He would shout "milk" in a very loud voice and the children would shout back "and water".

Grandma was not particularly fond of their two dogs but aunt Janie and Nellie spoiled them dreadfully. They always had one or two dogs travelling with them, which seemed to live to a great age and to have had more than one noteworthy adventure. One escaped from a truck on the railway. Aunt Janie told me they had fastened Laddie in the shooting gallery wagon which was

Aunt Nellie with a Winchester Rifle from the Shooting Gallery, and Aunt Janie holding the baby. Uncle Jimmy's twin daughters Jane and Ellen are standing.

Henshaw's road Living Wagon. This was also built by the local wagon building firm of Pollits at Bolton.

being sent by rail, but he had got out onto the railway lines when they were moving from Cadishead to Widnes. The family were en route with their road wagon, and they had Willie's dog with them. It kept barking as they were travelling alongside the railway lines and Laddie must have heard the barking and went down to the road where they were reunited. This was a great relief to aunt Janie who had got the station master to wire all the lines to look out for him. Another, getting loose in the same manner, arrived some time later at their house in Heywood where Butterworths, their kindly neighbours, took him in and let my aunts know of his arrival.

One was a real hero, seeing a bolting horse careering wildly down the street, he jumped on the dangling reins and held on until further help came. This merited mention in the local paper, of which my aunts were very proud.

But noble, heroic and warrior dogs as they were, they were invariably spoilt by my aunts' pampering and petting, for the dogs became their main objects of affection. When they were in the house they were always yapping, and barking and racing

through the house out of the back door to a football field, then round the house and in through the front door. My aunts worshipped them.

My mother was also a dog lover and I remember when our poor old "Nigger", a Black Russian Retriever, had to be put down (he was over 17 years old), she wept bitterly and could not be comforted.

We always enjoyed going to grandma Henshaw's, and it was a second home to us. Grandmother was a strong woman of Irish extraction, and she had auburn hair. Her grandparents, the Kellys, had come over from Dublin in the early part of the 19th century. Her grandfather (Kelly) had been a tailor who had been very proud of the fact that he had made Lady Byron's riding habit. We were told that one of our great grandmother's sisters had been the youngest headmistress appointed in Lancashire and was only twenty seven when she was appointed. Her parents William and Mary (nee Byrne) were married at the Catholic Church of St.Michael and All Angels, Stockport. I can recall as a child seeing Mary, my great-grandmother. She seemed very sprightly and lived on her own in a house in Manchester. I know my mother visited her and took groceries. Grandmother was very lively and witty. She would dance an Irish jig for us but we had to dance for her too. When she was eighty she danced a jig with me, arms akimbo and toe to knee. She had all her teeth and could thread a needle without the help of glasses. Although her auburn hair had lost its glorious colour she was still dynamic in her outlook. My grandmother met and married young William Henshaw while they were both in their teens. The ceremony was conducted at Manchester Cathedral. They started travelling the fairs and had swings, shooting galleries, emmas and coconut shies, but grandfather Henshaw was no businessman. He could quote Shakespeare at great length and frequently did so. He took a great interest in politics (he was a Tory) and would disappear for days on end during an election. He was beloved by his children and his workpeople, but DRINK, the demon king of the 19th century, lured him from prosperity, and had it not been for my energetic grandmother, disaster would most surely have overtaken the family. Grandmother was not the loveable type. She worked hard, ate heartily, feared no one and spoke her mind and expected others to do the same. Her gentlemanly husband must have infuriated her, especially as he refused to quarrel, and in an age when wife beating was customary, neither chided nor touched her or the children. Perhaps she took too much on her shoulders. A little more responsibility might have changed her husbands lightness of heart, but be that as it may, grandfather Henshaw went his merry way, loved and beloved until he died on 21st September 1894 age 54.

Grandmother was a great walker. My aunts told me more than once she walked from Wigan to Chester (30 miles) and when my brother Tom was born she walked from Heywood to Oldham (8 miles) despite being 73. She was anxious to see how mother and the baby were getting along. Tom was the only one born in a caravan, which was on the Tommyfield Market, Oldham. Like myself Billy was born in Hulme, Manchester, but at a different address, 118 Welcomb Street. On Billy's birth certificate my father is described as a "swing boat and merry-go-round proprietor". My two sisters were born in the house at Heywood.

Grandmother died in 1919, aged eighty two. Five of her children survived to become adults.

Mother in front of our living van nursing our new sister May. I am to mother's left side with Janie standing in front of me.

Mother and Aunt Nellie.

Auntie Nellie was kind and loveable and very like mother in appearance. Her sister Janie was quite different. She was small and had a deformed back. This was caused by falling from a back seat at the circus, but as she had been forbidden to go, she was too frightened to tell her mother. When it became obvious that something was wrong, she was taken to a Salford hospital and had to lie on hard boards for months. However as her health did not improve, grandma took her home, where she was given good nourishing food and plenty of rest. The back never straightened, but Janie was strong and recovered, and could still work like a man. Up and down ladders, fixing lights for the stalls and shooting galleries. Building up and pulling down the equipment which had to be dismantled or erected at each fair.

Henshaws attended the same fairs for seventy years. They were well known to their customers, who knew they would get fair treatment. These regulars would usually leave with ornamental metal birds on their caps to how the world they had won a prize. They had various types of stalls, some were called "Emmas", at which customers threw hard wooden balls at heads, and if they knocked teeth down, this counted as a win. They had to regularly buy "swag", the term used for prizes given on the fairground. The swag dealers' shops were mostly in Shudehill, Manchester, near the old Henmarket. Once my aunts sent a nephew, young Willie Taylor, from Liverpool to Manchester to buy some doves which were very popular at the time. They anticipated a good evening's business, so they impressed upon the boy the urgent need for his early return. "Come back on the very next train" Willie was told, and he arrived in Manchester in somewhat of a flurry. It was his first important errand. Obeying instructions, he asked a porter what time the next train would leave for Liverpool. "Why" said the porter, "There's one in now. Hurry up and you will catch it." So John Willie rushed for the train, caught it and arrived back in Liverpool in record time but minus the swag. My aunts were not amused.

Henshaws also had shooting galleries with Winchester rifles and live ammunition. Auntie

Nellie was a good shot and adept at coaxing people to have a go. Henshaw's "Tube Shooter" was a popular attraction. On this the customer shot at a cardboard target at the end of a long broad steel tube. On their other shooting gallery the customers shot at celluloid balls dancing on jets of water.

My mother (prior to getting married) and her two sisters loved the theatre and would do almost anything to be able to attend the delights of a romantic play etc. They even sold their mother's best dress, with dire consequences for them, in order to have enough money for a theatre visit.

The three sisters were dispatched from a fairground in the vicinity of Manchester to go into the City and buy some boxes of gunpowder for the Winchester shooter. Having made their purchase they duly visited the theatre. The three sisters blissfully sucked oranges in the gallery, lost in dreams of Romeo and Juliet, and with enough gunpowder under their seats to blow up half the neighbourhood.

During the winter months Henshaw's fairground equipment was parked in a big yard at the back of the house with a high black fence giving it privacy. In this yard were stables for three horses and there was room in the yard for three caravans and trucks.

Grandma's next door neighbour (No.12) was Joe Butterworth who was also a travelling showman and he shared the yard with her. He operated a pea saloon, which was a booth where you could sit down and enjoy brown peas in a thin soup into which you sprinkled vinegar. These peas are also known as black peas or parched peas.

Mother told me that grandma had her own way of sweeping the chimney. She would take a Winchester rifle from her shooting gallery and fire it up the chimney and so bring down all the soot. This was done when she "turned in" after a season's travelling and she spent every winter at home in Heywood.

Nellie and Janie retired around 1930 and lived at 10 Collinge St. for the rest of their lives. Janie died in 1954 age eighty four and Nellie in 1957 age eighty six.

Joe Butterworth's 'Noted' Pea Saloon. Butterworths owned No.12 Collinge Street, next door to Grandma Henshaw, and their fairground equipment was packed away for the winter in the shared yard at the back of the two houses.

UNCLE JIMMY HENSHAW

The twins, Jane and Ellen Henshaw in front of the family Tube Shooter. The showfront is folded out from the side of a Living Wagon, and the two firing tubes pass through and beyond the wagon to the target boxes.

Mother's brother uncle Jimmy, the only boy, was grandma's pride and joy. He would drink a quart of milk and eat half a loaf of bread for his breakfast. He was a great fighter and had inherited his mother's temper and red hair, plus his father's fecklessness. He was married at sixteen and was the father of nineteen children by his wife Mary. Before he was twenty he had five children.

When uncle Jimmy's younger set of twins were about two weeks old, they were brought to Wigan Fair to visit their grandmother, who was open on the Market Place with swings and her shooting gallery. "Have they been christened?" was grandma's first question and, on being told that they had not, insisted on two young women who worked for her, and who lived in Wigan, taking the babies to the Parish Church to have them christened. The babies were identical twins and I could never tell them apart. Grandma fastened a blue ribbon round the arm of the baby to be named

Jane and a pink ribbon round the other twin to be named Ellen. The young women and the babies were away for over two hours and the family were getting anxious when they eventually rolled up. "Rolled up" is a correct description. The godparents had had the babies christened and then had called in a nearby pub, where they had well and truly "wet the babies heads".

The identical twins had caused quite a sensation with drinks all round. It was Wigan Fair Week and a time of general rejoicing. Unfortunately, by the time they returned to grandma, the ribbons identifying Jane from Ellen had been lost and no one ever knew which one was christened Ellen and which one Jane. Grandma was furious, but when the twins were old enough to understand what had happened, they thought it a wonderful idea and one which apparently made them feel closer to each other.

Not only were the twins similar in appearance

My brother Billy left, cousin Benny Mitchell, and seated uncle Jimmy Henshaw outside an elaborate road or rail Living Wagon. It is likeley that this was also built by Pollits of Bolton. There is a tradional water can or carrier on the footboard.

with golden hair, blue eyes and pink and white complexions, but even when they were miles apart, each knew when the other was ill. They married, one lived in Southport and one in Rochdale, but were never content when away from each other. Eventually they and their husbands happily shared a house in Southport.

Ellen (Rhodes) died when she was eighty four. Jane (Clayton) was very distressed. I took her to the funeral but she would not go near the grave. She sat in the church talking to Ellen in quite a normal voice but saying, "I won't be long Ellen, I will soon be with you." She died around a fortnight later on 23rd July 1961.

Uncle Jimmy was certainly feckless but unlike his father, lacking in charm. Time and again his mother had to rescue him out of financial difficulties. At times he would drive his wife and children almost to despair. He was however a skilled joiner and a good painter but after beer and whisky he was to be avoided at all costs by anyone of peaceable inclinations.

Once he decided to try his luck on the Scottish fairs but this proved disastrous. However, he managed to "raise the wind" sufficiently to pay for his caravan to be sent home by rail, by goods train, and for his own fare back. The caravan was put upon a railway truck and the chimney taken off in order to allow free passage under bridges. As the journey was to take only one day and as uncle Jimmy was by now completely without money, he locked his collie dog inside the caravan with an adequate supply of food and water. He then travelled to Wigan by passenger train where he arranged to meet the goods train and then take his wagon home to Heywood.

Imagine his horror when an irate station master demanded the dog's fare too, as becoming bored with the long journey, and being of an inquisitive nature, the dog had mounted the stove, pushed his head through the hole usually occupied by the chimney and was barking a joyful solo to the Wigan station master's personnel. Uncle Jimmy's remarks were remembered for many years.

A Showman's traction engine lowering a Living Wagon onto a flat railway carriage truck. Most stations had special railway docks with ramps for this procedure. (Copyright National Railway Museum).

37

Aunt Nellie, as usual with two of her beloved dogs.

After his wife Mary died, and when he was in his fifties, uncle Jimmy married Georgina, a widow from Bury. Sadly after only a short period of matrimony she became ill and died.

Jimmy suffered from asthma and this got worse as he got older. After his second wife died it became most severe so he went to see a doctor in Bury who told him that he could only expect to live for another six months. Fortune had favoured him for the previous two years and he decided not to leave any money for anyone else to enjoy. So live and laugh those six months he did, beerily, happily and without thought of his impending doom. After six months his money had gone and death seemed no nearer. He went to see his two spinster sisters at the family house at Heywood. He explained his situation and they told him he could live with them. He was a good handyman for them assisting in their travelling business, and they did not regret it. While he lived at Heywood his children visited him.

I can remember his son Billy coming round to see grandma when I was there. Billy was very good with horses, and as grandma had one she was anxious about, she asked him to look at its feet. This he did and after a few minutes examination he put me on its back and walked it slowly up and down the street. I was so far from the ground that I had the impression that I was riding an elephant. Billy laughed and took me back to grandma and put the horse in the stable.

Billy and his younger brother Tommy were in the army during the First World War. Billy was in charge of horses, which is what he had hoped for. He was killed near Arras, Northern France, on 2nd. September 1918. Tommy returned home to his family after the war.

In the twenties mother, aunt Nellie, my sister Janie and I visited Billy's grave at St. Martin-sur-Cojeul near Arras. There were hundreds of identical graves of British soldiers from all walks of life and Billy's just one of them.

Uncle Jimmy continued to be looked after and cared for by his thrifty sisters. He died in the house at Collinge St. in February 1929 age sixty five. This family house witnessed the births and deaths of so many members of my family

Aunt Janie, probably filling water carriers, as she is holding the lid of a traditional showmans water can.

FAIRGROUND SHOWS I SAW THROUGHOUT MY LIFE

The paraders on the showfront of Proctor's Circus attracting an audience at a fair at Stockport in 1914.

I loved going to the circus. My favourite was Proctor's, as they were often on the same grounds as ourselves. Colonel Clark was the grandfather of four of my cousins, and whenever his show was on one of the fairgrounds we attended, we were frequent visitors. Occasionally my cousin Lucy would be allowed to appear dressed up as an angel. At the end of the performance and wired up to some mechanism she would fly gracefully across the stage. I was consumed with bitter jealousy, as I was never allowed to do this.

When we were at one big fair, I remember waking up and hearing the roar of lions. Looking through the bedroom window I could see an elephant being led to a tank of drinking water. It was so calm and steady in its walk that there was no sense of fear as it came near. Mother said they belonged to a circus, which had arrived early that morning, and I could go and see them when the fair was open. Later that day I saw several of the circus ponies being washed with soapy water and swilled down with clear water. They seemed to enjoy it, as did the small boys who lay on a double decked truck watching.

Some of the shows were really magnificent, with ornate gilded carved fronts and beautiful organs, which we thought played to perfection. A number of girls would parade on the front while the showman would call out, "Roll up, roll up" to the crowd, inviting them to the show. When the organ played "God Save the King", that was a sure sign that the show was about to start and the audience hurried to enter. There were many shows travelling the fairs. Melodrama was very popular in those days and, as most of the audiences were unsophisticated, this generally delighted the crowd. The line from "East Lynne", "Dead and never called me mother", caused oceans of tears to be shed in Lancashire. Some of our own fairground children would occasionally take part, but I was not one of the lucky ones. One of our friends in the cast had to declare in emotional tones, "And my father beats me every day." Her father was in the audience and shouted back, "That's a downright lie. I've never touched her in my life."

I can remember seeing a giant "strong man" who could bend six inch nails with his bare hands. In another part of his act he would put a blacksmith's anvil on his chest and let someone hit it with a large hammer. Sometimes he would support several men

Travelling Menageries were the only places that most people would ever have the chance of seeing exotic animals, these shows regularly opened alongside the attractions at larger fairs.

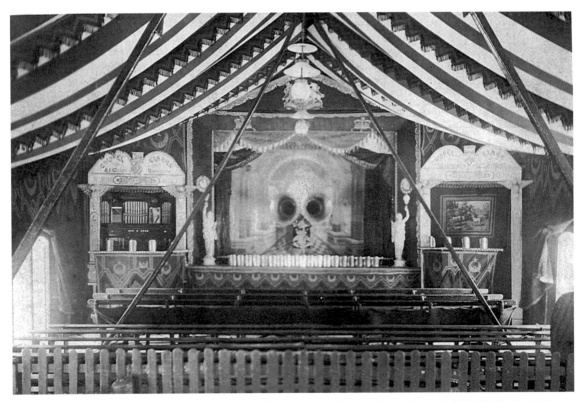

A post card view of the inside of Clark's Ghost Show. The back of the card reads:"The new Interior of Col. W. Clark's Exhibition. Presented June 7th 1905". The spectacle presented was also known as "Pepper's Ghost" after the inventor of the illusion, which used a piece of tilted glass in front of the stage to reflect images of the "Ghosts".

on a plank.

My favourite show was the "Ghost Show". This was an act put on by Colonel Clark's two sons, Sammy and Solly. It kept the audience screaming with laughter and fear. I found out later that this act was afterwards used in a number of Variety West End shows, performed by stars in a modern version. The Ghost Show lost its appeal when the showmen started travelling cinema shows. Very few country people had ever been to a cinema, so that the coming of films on the fairground caused quite a sensation. A number of showmen made the films themselves, their staff and families acting with gusto. The silent films were only short one-reel affairs, mostly comedies, though when the First World War started "Killing the Kaiser" was a regular feature. The bioscope shows vanished from the fairgrounds with the establishing of permanent cinemas. Many showmen had cinemas built and prospered as picture house owners.

Attractions on the fairground included a stall where you could buy nougat and toffee, watching it being made before you bought. There was ice cream too, with raspberry flavouring, and in one town (I think it was Accrington) you could buy ice cream and cream. I have never tasted better. The fortune tellers (sometimes Italian women) used to have budgies (or love birds as they called them) in a cage. These were trained to select leaflets to hand to the fortune seeker There was also a fortune teller, who had what we called a "tick off". This consisted of a card, which would give details of your character, and future events which you could look forward to. The fortune teller would mark your "reading" and there were always laughs and giggles from the girls as they read their future. I remember my sister Janie buying one of these cards when she was six. She was told she would live to be eighty and would marry a sailor. I remember my father was most annoyed at this waste of money. Auntie Janie told me that our fortune teller was not really a gypsy, her mother was Irish and her father was a "blackamoor" (a dark skinned person), an expression I had never heard before.

Besides the large elaborate shows there were sometimes quite small ones. I remember seeing a Red Indian who could lift a cannon with his teeth. He had an elaborate feathered head-dress, a mahogany coloured complexion and the most piercing blue eyes I have ever seen. Then there was a tiny little lady, "Anita, the Living Doll". She was seated in a beautifully made miniature trap, pulled by a Shetland pony. I also watched the man with elastic skin. He would get hold of the skin of his neck below his chin and would pull it out to a length of ten inches.

Another show was "A Fat Lady" and "The Ugliest Woman in Britain". Very popular was Al Capone's bulletproof car, which was exhibited on fairgrounds for a while and which attracted a lot of attention, particularly at big fairs. I remember seeing a tattooed man and a tattooed lady, they were covered with tattoos which completely altered their features.

When I was a child, I was quite bewildered by the "illusion shows". These included "The Headless Lady" and "The Spider Lady". There was also a "Petrified Man" billed as a human body which had turned to stone. This had, according to the owner, been found in an underground cavern.

This publicity post card shows one of several 'smallest women in the world' who were popular attractions in side shows for many years. (John White).

41

The Corporation of one town where this "Petrified Man" was taken said that an inquest should be held and the body given a Christian burial. Fearing the loss of his prize exhibit, neither the owner nor the body was to be found the following day.

The Kie (or Kaw) Shows were well known. These had coloured "wild men", discovered in the Jungle, who had been brought to England in a cage. They ran on all fours, grimacing, whilst making guttural noises and shaking their fists at the audience. They absolutely terrified me and I was always glad to get out and away from them.

Sometimes there was a diving show on the fairground and I enjoyed going to it, watching the diver, sometimes a man, sometimes a girl, diving and doing acrobatics under water. Then the diver would eat a banana while under water. This was something I could never understand, but it was done regularly and was a very popular act. There were a number of animal shows. The six-legged horse which was billed "The Norfolk Spider", and also the sheep with six legs. "Billy the Pig" was a freak because he was a true giant of the animal world and so much larger than a normal pig. The showman who owned this came from South Africa

but stayed in England for a number of years. The snake show always fascinated me. A girl would have huge snakes, including a python occasionally, and she would seem perfectly at ease when they were winding themselves around her body.

The flea circus was also a source of interest. Fleas were harnessed with a tiny wire and they pulled little carriages. The star of the flea circus was sometimes given a continental name such as Madame Rosa or Mademoiselle Carmen. The monkey shows generally kept the children amused, but mother told me not to go too near the bars, as she had once had her hair tugged very violently when she was a child and it only released her when the owner hit it with a cane. I can recall a show that exhibited a "Giant Octopus" which was really an India rubber version that breathed by means of a mechanical pump.

A working model of a coalmine showed a cross section thropugh the mine, which was an interesting and successful exhibit in another show.

One act I recall in a show was the "second sight" one, in which a blindfolded man could identify an object borrowed from the audience and held up by his assistant.

A 'wild man' taking time off from a 'Kie' show belonging to Buller Westray of Bradford. Westray was the lion tamer in the show. They are posed alongside the Foden steam wagon which was used for transport and accommodation. The lettering on the wagon states the maximum speed of 5 m.p.h.

SALFORD

When my brother Billy was five and I was nearly three, we were taken by mother to stay with great aunt Annie who lived in Salford. She kept a tiny corner shop in Sunnyside Street and sold sweets and groceries. Customers would come in and ask for a pennyworth of matches and were given four boxes.

Old women in shawls would ask for a "screw" of tea at a halfpenny a time. This was a small sheet of paper screwed into a bag and filled with tea.

There was a corner in the shop into which sanctuary I would sometimes flee from my brother. I well remember him caging me in a fireguard, and using a poker through the bars insisting that I was a lion and he the trainer. My screams brought my aunt to the rescue. Billy was a lively, irrepressible, intelligent, fearless child, who evoked my admiration and terror. Billy tried her sorely. I think she secretly thought him a limb of Satan, but to me she was kind and gentle. My doll's cream jug and sugar basin were displayed in her glass cabinet along with her own treasured china. She washed and polished them with as much ceremony as her own.

She was a small thin featured woman, between 50 and 60, with her hair parted in the middle and drawn tightly to the back in a tiny bun. She was religious and texts were on the walls of every room in the house.

My aunt, who had been married four times, was a widow. She seemed to have no interest in remembering her late husbands, except for the last one, uncle Tom. His photograph was displayed on the mantelpiece because apparently he had been a model of all the virtues. The other three were veiled in mystery and my aunt gave us the impression that the less said the better.

She had two sons. Jack Burroughs, the elder, who was married, would play lugubriously on the small harmonium in the living room when he visited. He was later given a civic reception when he returned home at the end of the First World War, and was considered quite a hero by the family. Tom Finney, the younger son, was a bachelor with a cheerful outlook and endeavoured to teach Billy to swim. Billy, full of confidence, dived in at the first attempt and cut his head so badly that the lessons were abandoned.

Sunnyside Street was a typical Salford working class street. The houses were four roomed: two bedrooms, a living room and a scullery. The people were decent, hardworking employees of the lower paid class. There were plenty of children in Sunnyside Street and although the neighbourhood was drab and even dreary the pulse of life seemed rich, interesting and crammed with vitality. When my mother visited us in a cab swarms of children would appear from every side. I remember the feeling of tremendous importance I felt on such occasions.

Although aunt Annie sold toffees Billy knew of a shop where more could be bought for a penny. One could emerge with an assortment of four different types of sweets in four separate bags, and all for a copper coin, the Saturday penny. Billy, knowing no loyalty where sweets were concerned, took his own and his friends custom there.

Billy and I during our schooldays at Salford.

43

Billy and I had gone to auntie's, because it was compulsory for children to attend school at five and the teachers were also quite willing to admit me, though under age, as a pupil. Auntie took us to school and it seemed a long way to walk. She left me with a small bag of oatmeal and sugar while Billy had a bag of sherbet and a liquorice stick through which one could suck the sherbet, or kaly, as we called it then. Billy was taken into one classroom and I went into another. Nobody spoke to me but all the other children were reciting something I could not understand. Prayers, no doubt, but not the ones I knew. Thoroughly miserable, I started to cry. This galvanised the teacher into activity. "Stop at once," she yelled. As I continued to sob, she shouted, "If you don't stop this minute, I'll hang you on the gas bracket." This had two big white globes, one at each end, and hung from the ceiling. I continued crying (I had never been spoken to like that before) and a few minutes later my brother Billy was brought into the classroom with orders to make me behave.

"What's the matter?" asked Billy. "The teacher says she is going to hang me," I sobbed. "Don't be silly," said Billy. "She won't, you know. If she hangs you our grandad will hang her, and our Daddy will hang her and our uncle Bennie will hang her and uncle Willie will hang her. Nobody will hang you. When you come out at playtime I will be waiting for you and you can tell me if anyone has been nasty." I was quite pacified. Billy had convinced me that I was in no danger and that I had him to meet in the playground soon afterwards.

The teacher brought me a tray of sand and a stick about six inches long. "You must make an O like an orange," she told me. "Just watch me." I did and found that I could do the same, reciting "O like an orange" for at least half an hour. When the bell went and we all marched into the playground. Billy was already there, turning somersaults. When I told him that everything was all right and nobody had threatened or hurt me, he looked really disappointed. Not that Billy really cared. He upset me far more than all the others, but he dearly loved a fight and was glad of any excuse.

After some time at school and when I had done all the letters of the alphabet in the sand and knew them all, I was given a large sheet of stiff cardboard perforated with holes and a long red bootlace. With this I was shown how to make letters, capital letters now, threading the bootlace in and out quite easily.

I soon knew all the capital letters. Later I was given a slate and a slate pencil, copying letters and words on the blackboard, then wiping them off with a damp cloth. There was no waste paper and no untidy desks. The bigger girls would collect the slates at the end of the lesson and put them in a cupboard. At long last I was given a book and a pencil with words at the top of each page to copy. These words were beautifully done, but they bore no relation to the work I turned out. However, I could read quite well before I was five and could also write a card home to my parents not long afterwards.

It was quite an adventure coming out of school. The children seemed to gang up and other gangs would stop us and say, "Proddidogs or Catlicks?" According to your answer you had to beat a hasty retreat or gang up with the others. Billy and I were Catholics and went to a Catholic school where our fellow pupils seemed well able to take care of themselves.

Sunday was quite different from any other day of the week. We wore our best Sunday clothes, and Billy and I went to Mass at the Catholic Church about half a mile away from auntie's. Billy went to Holy Communion, which meant that he was not allowed to eat or drink anything before the service. I had breakfast, and while I was eating it, Billy would go to a huge earthenware bowl with a wooden lid on top which contained bread. He would help himself to a slice of bread and butter, which he would later eat on his way home. The Mass, said in Latin, was a complete mystery to me. I couldn't see the priest or the altar and would usually sit on a kneeler, which I found was more comfortable than the hard bench. As I couldn't see anything, I used to listen to the singing, most of which was in Latin, and just waited for the time when Billy said we could leave.

When we got back to auntie's, we had a meal, but we were reminded that it was Sunday and we must not sing in the house. Sunday was a day of prayer, but I quite liked it because it had more variety than the other days. After Mass at the Catholic Church on Sunday morning, auntie Maria called for me in the afternoon and took me to the Salvation Army Citadel. Maria was always dressed in black. She had a black poked bonnet, a black cape and a black skirt, which she told me had thirty six yards of black braid sewn round it in circles. I liked the Salvation Army. They had a brass band

Henry Powell's manually propelled bicycle ride at Hull Fair before the First War. People were happy to pay one penny for the novelty of being able to ride on a bicycle at a time when most people could not afford one of their own.

and everyone sang with great gusto. I could soon join in, my favourite being "My sins were as high as the mountain, they all disappeared in the fountain".

When the service was over, auntie Maria took me home to tea and after that auntie Annie got me ready for "The Mission". This was a splendid place with a wonderful atmosphere. When they had a Harvest Festival, fruit and vegetables were piled up on the altar and flowers were there in abundance. The clergyman was kind and always talked to me after the service, when I would recite "Gentle Jesus". When we got back home it was usually my bedtime, but if Jack was visiting his mother he would play the harmonium and we could sing - hymns of course! I really liked the Mission and the Salvation Army and had nothing but kindness from members of the congregation, but at school the teacher was so lurid in her description of Hell and Hell Fire that I started having nightmares, screaming loudly during the night. I can still remember seeing the leaping flames that terrified me. One morning, after such a night, auntie sent for the doctor. What he advised I don't know, but I think I had a week or two away from school and the teacher seemed to tone down her description of the

Devil and Hell Fire afterwards.

Billy was never bored in Sunnyside Street. When every other game palled he would hide his shoes and stockings and go out with bare footed newsboys selling papers or even stand outside the huge mill and beg for the left over "butties" which the workmen sometimes handed to the waiting children. I can see him now with his dark curly hair, ruddy cheeks glowing with health and his short sturdy legs, a little tough guy among the pale, spindle shanked children around him.

My aunt fed us and looked after us well and gave us our weekly bath and senna pods every Saturday night, followed by a sweet to "take the taste away." Whatever parents or grown ups told me to do, I did.

How I hated the senna pods. Billy, on the other hand, enjoyed the brew. Billy would swallow mine (if my aunt happened to go out of the room) provided he had the sweet as well. Many a time he had a double dose and I had none without my aunt being any the wiser. Occasionally Billy and I would visit Janie, (third of the family) who lived with "aunt" Hannah Vaughan about half a mile away. Janie was very happy there. The house was bright and cheerful and Hannah, who had two boys of her own, was obviously delighted to have a little girl to take care of. I remember the first time I went to tea there. There were cakes, biscuits, thin bread and butter and jam. There was also something I had never had before, pineapple chunks and custard. I think this was the first tinned fruit to be brought to England and the sweet crunchy flavour was delicious. Long white starched curtains draped the windows. There was no praying or hymn singing, as at Annie's. Janie had her hair arranged in stiff Victorian curls and wore very starched white pinafores. She had short sight and had silver round glasses. My aunt viewed such vanity with distaste and as the work of the devil. When I first entered her household, at the age of almost three, she plaited my curls into little pigtails securing them with cotton at the ends. Then she lengthened my dresses so that they reached well below the knee. It was her idea of what was fitting for a little girl.

Two songs seemed to be sung a great deal in those days, "Everybody's Doing It" and "Alexander's Rag Time Band".

On Saturday afternoons we went to the Pictures (a children's matinee). Hundreds of screaming children were packed inside, waiting for a white dot to appear. Claps and cheers would herald the start of the programme. Sometimes we were given an orange and a comic paper as we went in. I think the charge was 3d. but it may have been even less.

The games the children played in the street were sometimes rough and noisy. In one particular war game the children would split into two camps: one, the "English", which everyone wanted to join, and the enemy, the "French", which those who had not been selected were obliged to join. The English headquarters backed onto a wall and, when the signal "charge" was given, the two sides rushed at each other, tried to take prisoners and, when they had done, marched them back to headquarters, where they had to remain until the end of the game. Dresses, shirts and blouses were often torn and there was usually trouble at home afterwards for all the warriors. This battle only took place once a year, but what it was supposed to commemorate I really don't know.

Another annual event was Guy Fawkes Night, when one big bonfire was lit in the street and fireworks were let off. We had treacle toffee and, after having our hands tied at the back, tried to bite apples on a string and win the apple when we dislodged it. We also had apples in a bowl of water

and again had to bite an apple in order to win it. Hair dripping, eyes streaming, we thought it wonderful.

On May Day there were processions of little girls attending the May Queen, who carried flowers and had a wreath and veil. The other little girls were in long dresses, their hair washed and curled with satin ribbons woven into a wreath on their heads. The houses were decorated with ribbons and brasses that shone.

The usual street games seemed to run to a pattern. At the first spring day skipping ropes would appear and "salt, mustard, vinegar, pepper" was a chant to be heard far and wide. Then there was "hopscotch", the plan being mapped out in chalk and always the same pattern. The boys played "bobbin and spoons" and "marbles" and a sort of leap-frog game, a few of them running and jumping on the leader's back. Another skipping rope game was "higher and higher", where two girls would hold a rope and other girls would line up and jump over it, the rope being held higher and higher each time. The first girl to fall had to hold the rope and allow the girl she replaced to join the line of jumpers.

Once tragedy overtook Sunnyside Street. A well loved child died and I was taken to see the body. It's waxy little face with two pennies on its eyes sent a shock of horror through me such as I have never experienced and the acrid smell of death smote my nostrils unexpectedly. I have other memories of Sunnyside Street. Of going to school with a paper bag containing oatmeal and sugar, or cocoa and sugar and sometimes a bag of currants. My aunt sold aniseed balls at twelve a penny. These were surely the most delicious and interesting of all sweets, to be licked and looked at many times before dissolving.

We were never allowed out when it was dark. Auntie insisted on that. I knew the other children in the street and used to play with them, but, as soon as the sky began to darken, I rushed home. When I asked the reason for this, auntie would say there were wicked men in the world, who would lure us away and strip us of our clothes, which they would sell. I was terrified at the idea of being left without clothes but Billy couldn't have cared less. As far as he was concerned, clothes were a nuisance and, if he could lose them forever, that would have suited him nicely. He once came in with his trousers torn and, when asked what happened, he said quite seriously that the wind had done it. Everyone laughed, but it seemed quite logical to me. When we were at home on the fairground, our parents were always afraid that the roundabout's tilts (or canvas covers) would be torn by the wind and they occasionally were. A travelling tailor with a special sewing machine would call and repair them.

My aunt never punished or smacked us though her threats were extreme, "I'll saw your leg off" was used so often that it had very little effect or meaning. "I'll whip you within an inch of your life" left us unmoved. Had she deprived us of the rich creamy golden skinned rice pudding, for which she was noted, then indeed she might have achieved more satisfactory results.

On one occasion my father visited Salford bringing a cricket bat, ball and wickets for Billy and a doll for myself. Unfortunately we were not to be found and my father had to leave without seeing us. That day we had gone to Peel Park and spent glorious hours in a shallow pond. I was sitting on a huge stone in the middle with my shoes and socks off. Billy was doing battle with all and sundry.

However that was the end of our stay in Sunnyside Street. My father who was a good Catholic decided that what was needed was more orderly supervision and different surroundings. He therefore arranged for my mother to take Billy to the Salesian College (a boarding school) in Hampshire, and I was to attend a convent at Monks Kirby, about seven miles north west of Rugby, in Warwickshire. When my mother told me that I would soon be going to a convent boarding school, I was very upset. I explained to my mother, "They don't know me, mammy, and perhaps they won't like me."

"Well, they will, when they get to know you. When you first meet them, tell them that your family has two yachts, eight motor cars and forty eight jumping horses. That will interest them, at least. If ever we go to any town where they live, they can all have free rides."

Mitchell's eight Motor Cars on the Switchback ride travelled by Uncle Willie.

SAINT JOSEPH'S CONVENT

My sister Janie (front row third from the right) and fellow pupils at Saint Joseph's Convent.

Then followed a hectic time of clothes buying and the sewing on each of my garments of a nametape, "Eleanor Mitchell". Up to then I had been "Nellie" and I don't think I even knew my name was Eleanor.

My mother took me to the convent. It was the longest train journey I had ever been on, and when we eventually reached our station it was to find that we were several miles from the school and that there was no public transport of any kind. The nearest cabby lived in a village two miles away. However there was a Railway Inn and there my mother and I waited until a horse and cab eventually appeared and took us to the convent.

Down long quiet roads we drove with flat fields on every side, cattle grazing, and trees in plenty. I was completely surprised. I had never seen or visualised such loneliness, such utter emptiness. How could I ever exist in such surroundings? The lack of human activity frightened me.

When we arrived at the convent we rang a bell which we could hear clanging in the distance and a nun in black appeared, to open the door. She welcomed us quietly and with large rosary beads

clinking showed us into the little parlour to wait for the Reverend Mother. We did not have to wait long, and she and my mother were soon having a friendly chat. I realised that she was Irish. She assured us that I would be quite happy with the other girls and that my mother was not to fret or worry, I would be well taken care of.

I do not remember my mother leaving nor do I remember much of my first day there, except that it seemed to me that the house was enormous and the floors unending, miles of cold dark shining unfriendly linoleum. The light walls were decorated only sparsely with holy pictures and in the corners of many of the rooms were vividly painted statues of Christ, His Mother or Saint Joseph. I felt deserted, alone in an alien world. I was six and this was the second time in my short life I had been uprooted.

But the big outside world claimed us. "Education" was the stick used to beat us out of our nest. First of all to the day school at Salford, where we had lived with my great aunt and now to the convent where I was to spend eight long and sometimes dreary but nevertheless profitable years.

48

The convent was in or adjacent to the Earl of Denbigh's estate. He had considerable influence in the area and was a local benefactor. The nuns were kind and were from the Order of St.Vincent de Paul, which was based in The Hague, Holland. The convent itself came as a great shock to me. The rooms were always cold and the food was dreadful.

How can I convey the convent atmosphere? The refectory, in which we ate and played, had one long table and benches at either side running the length of the room. Two oil lamps hung suspended from the ceiling and on the wall were two large paintings, one of the "Sacred Heart" and the other of "Our Lady". At the end of the room was a fireplace and a large dark oak cupboard in which we kept our books.

We had cake every Sunday at teatime and I can still savour its fruity flavours. Gastronomically, it was the highlight of the week. Friday was the day I dreaded, as on that day the midday meal consisted of tinned salmon and breadcrumbs, the smell of which caused my stomach to heave. By holding my nose and swallowing rapidly I managed weekly to dispose of the abominable mess.

When my sisters Janie and May later became pupils at the convent, it made life easier. My cousin Lucy was also a boarder at this school. Fellow pupil Molly Coleman was a contemporary of Janie's at the convent. We both liked her and remained in touch as adults.

I was neither popular nor unpopular at the convent. I had my friends and enjoyed their company, but most of the time was spent in a make believe world of my own. I read hungrily without dissemination or discretion. Every available book that fell into my hands was read from cover to cover. As I discovered each one, so at the time, the characters became my friends, enemies or companions, their lives and loves, the absorbing interest of my life.

SCHOOL HOLIDAYS

Holidays were eagerly looked forward to throughout the year. We went home for five weeks, usually the last week in July until the last weekend in August.

Returning home from the convent for the summer holidays was sheer bliss. I was usually sick with excitement before we left, and on one occasion I fainted in the chapel before breakfast. I was terrified in case I was put to bed and not allowed to go home, but I think the nuns recognised that it was due to excitement. They took me to Rugby, where I was put on a train going direct to Manchester.

The contrast was a strange one and sometimes our caravan seemed cramped and small and the life on the fairground strange. But only when I got back to the fairground, our own caravan and family did I feel really at ease and happy, especially as the atmosphere was bright and friendly.

On holiday I loved to get on to the caravan roof, take off the steel chimney and hand it down to whoever was going to clean it. Quite a lot of soot accumulated in it every week which was then brushed out into a cardboard box and taken away by one of the workmen. When on the roof I always got a feeling of exhilaration and wanted to sing. To me it was as thrilling as being on top of Blackpool Tower. Everything looked so different. I would stay as long as I could, and as none of the other members of the family wanted to do this I had no competition. It was my first conscious feeling of freedom.

Billy had become a teenager, though school had changed him little. My father was still the same (strong, dark and bold) and my mother loving, kindly and protective as ever.

Although nearly all my relatives lived on the fairground, my aunt Tillie, (Matilda), who had married a showman, Jack Taylor, had subsequently left the business and now lived near Birkenhead. When I was about eleven years old and on holiday from the convent mother asked me if I would like to go to Liverpool to see her eldest sister? I was thrilled at the idea. When we arrived at Liverpool we took a tram to the Pier Head. These trams were quite different to the trams in Manchester or Preston, you could travel first or second class and mother bought first class tickets. I had never travelled first class before. When we arrived at the Pier Head I was absolutely enthralled, what a grand sight for a child who for 11 months of the year was buried in the country. The wide river teeming with craft of every description bound for America, Africa, India and the whole wide world and flanked by the impressive Liver and Cunard buildings. The seagulls screaming and dipping over the water and the covered gangway to the boats swaying gently at the dockside. Colonied men and Chinese mixed with the crowd, and the salt tanged air with the smell of fish and the indefinable aroma of a great seaport.

Mother said we would go on one of the ferries "across the water", which was the way locals talked of this trip. We boarded the boat for Rock Ferry and it rocked gently on the river. Most of the passengers seemed to be walking round in circles from the time we left until we arrived. As the ferryboat approached the south side of the river my mother pointed out aunty Tillie's bungalow, situated on the very edge of the River Mersey. An ordinary bungalow to outward appearances but inside completely apart. How different it was!

When the boat arrived the gangplank was lowered and mother and I set off for the bungalow. We knocked and could hear Tillie's voice. My aunt opened the door to us and her face lit up with pleasure, mother was the favourite with all her family. We were invited in, but this was easier said than done. My aunt had a passion for sale-rooms and blocking the door was a huge organ which even though dismantled filled the hall, so that mother and I had to squeeze through in order to pass. Tillie explained that there was only one other organ like it and that was in Blackpool Tower. In the parlour

was a stuffed leopard, (head raised and tail outstretched, poised in a menacing manner), two pianos, a Louis XIV cabinet, a small desk with a sloping leather top and several delicate spindly legged chairs with gold brocade covers. These filled the room, while every square inch of the walls was taken up with oil paintings, portraits, landscapes, and animal studies all hobnobbed together. Miniatures and larger than life pictures stared down at us.

Tillie advised that she was just going around the corner and would be back in a few minutes. She brought out her tricycle, donned a lavender cape and a motoring veil and off she went to the nearest shops. She came back with fresh bread, boiled ham, biscuits and cakes and we were soon eating and enjoying a meal.

The kitchen was less crowded with the inanimate but crowded with livestock: three cats, two dogs and a parrot shared this room. The parrot, grey and pink, chatted incessantly and easily - devoured a piece of bread and jam, an apple and a drink of tea. My uncle Jack talked to it lovingly, smoking his pipe and beaming at us with the most friendly air. Aunt Tillie at one sale had apparently

An Edwardian post card of the landing stage at Liverpool showing the Mersey ferries tied up waiting to take passengers across the river. The White Star liner "Oceanic" has just made or is about to make an Atlantic crossing. In the distance to the right the distinctive New Brighton tower can be seen.

50

been unable to resist a bargain of spittoons and as a consequence spittoons filled with sawdust were to be seen in the hearth and the corners of each room. The back yard disclosed still more treasures. Bicycles large and small filled the shed, and the tricycle was usually parked here. This was used by auntie Tillie for shopping and the basket at the back carried her purchases. Even Tillie's handbag showed evidence of her sale-room mania. Rings, brooches, pendants and matching earrings - valuable, cheap and tawdry - filled her bag. Each had a history. One had been bought at Chester another at Liverpool, still another at an auction held on an estate nearby. But each was a bargain and no seeker of gold took greater pride in their find than did my aunt.

However it was soon time to go and when we were on the boat we could see Tillie waving to us until we were out of sight. When we arrived back in Liverpool mother said she would take me on an Underground train. This was another thrill. It was lit up and I could not imagine how they could have managed such a marvellous thing. When we walked out of the Underground I saw the first black man I had ever seen, although I did not consider him black: he looked more purple to me. Mother told me not to stare as nobody liked being stared at, and that there were quite a lot of coloured people in Liverpool. We took the train back to Bolton where the fair and our caravan were. I told my father about our adventures and how I had enjoyed my visit to Liverpool.

"Did Tillie say how her son Albert was getting on?" asked my father. "Yes," said mother, "He's doing nicely and is now in Chicago." That was the end of a perfect day. After all the excitement of visiting Liverpool, I found that I had an unknown cousin in Chicago, America. Wonderful. (Albert prospered in Chicago. He married a girl called Jessie and they had two sons Claude and Charles. During the war Claude was a pilot of a B.17, Flying Fortress based in England. He was killed, age 21, over Berlin on 5th. December 1944. In 1949 his body was brought back to Chicago. Albert died in 1957 age 67. Albert, Jessie and Claude's graves are alongside each other in Chicago's Evergreen Cemetery.)

In the years that followed I got to know aunt Tillie well. Uncle Jack was a great disappointment to her and as a consequence, she sometimes neglected him. He once bought a pair of trousers which he complained were two inches too long. Tillie had other fish to fry at the time (salesrooms being more important than needlework) so for a fortnight, in spite of her husband's protests, the trousers remained un-shortened. Relenting one day she decided to shorten them and did so. Unfortunately daughter Beatrice was also in an energetic and kindly mood and not knowing that her mother had already "done the deed" sliced off another two inches. Uncle Jack had visited the local pub. His wife and daughter were to be taught a lesson. In short he would show them! He would shorten the trousers himself. So he promptly cut off another two inches and tacked the turn ups as best he could. The following day nobody was more surprised than uncle Jack. His trousers reached up to his calves and even the parrot was too stunned to utter his usual whistle.

Every subsequent holiday I visited Tillie and each time I was given a present. A piano, a bicycle, a set of golf clubs, always something too big to take away and always something invariably sold by the time I visited her on my next holiday. But then I would be given another present which would follow the fate of its predecessor. Poor Tillie, always so generous at heart, but somehow never quite reaching the heights. Tillie did all her own housework and looked after her invalid daughter Beatrice and two grandsons, George and Arthur (the latter had inherited his grandmother's red hair). At the age of 81 she made a cup of tea, sat down to drink it and died quietly.

When I came home for my summer holidays in July 1914 I had a first ride in a taxicab. I was eight, and mother's fifth child Thomas had been born in February that year. Mother brought our baby brother to London Road Station, Manchester, to meet us. It was a fine warm day and mother had hired an open taxi, so that we could cross Manchester in style. Previously we had always taken a horse drawn vehicle. Despite the snorts and jerks of the open taxicab, Janie and I were thrilled and were very disappointed when we reached our destination. Mother, bless her, promised us more rides and said that there were quite a lot of motor cars about now, but of course there would always be horses, and cars would never take their place. Mother loved horses. Her family had always owned them, and she and her sisters had ridden bareback as children and as young women.

The baby Tom was dressed for the occasion. He

The mechanical organ in Uncle Willie's electric Scenic Motor Car ride. This was an 87 key instrument built in Paris by the firm of Gavioli for Grandfather. It was previously used in the steam driven Motor Car Switchback ride. The electric lights were carbon arc lamps, the brilliant light created by electricity arcing between two carbon rods.

looked magnificent in a white embroidered dress and a cartwheel hat with a rim of broderie anglaise and yards of pale blue ribbon streamers. We drove through Manchester like royalty and visited aunt Annie's in Salford where I had lodged when attending my first school. Mother asked the driver to wait, we would only be about a quarter of an hour. Within a matter of seconds the taxi was surrounded by children, all inquisitive and asking questions. They had never seen a motor car in that street, at least not a car that stopped outside a house there.

We went into the house, which seemed very dark at first, and the harmonium was still in the front room.

Annie's dog, Peter, had died many years ago. She had him stuffed and he was kept in a glass case above the parlour door.

I was pleased to see that my greatest treasure, a doll's cut glass sugar basin and cream jug given to me on my sixth birthday, still occupied pride of place in her display cabinet. However, we soon had to leave, this time to catch another train to take us

to Accrington. The fair was due to open there and father was waiting anxiously for our arrival.

When we eventually arrived, mother took us to our caravan and put Tom, who was now asleep, on the top bed, with pillows round him to prevent him falling off.

We then took off our hats and coats and pointed to the traction engine "Shall I Do It" which our father was driving on the fairground. As soon as he saw us, father stopped the engine and lifted all three of us on to where the coal was stacked, kissed us and then set off immediately down the ground. Our Great Dane, Duchess, followed, leaping and barking with excitement.

It was heaven just to know we were back in the old familiar world and before the day was over we would be kissed and welcomed by grandfather and our many relatives and friends. It was marvellous just to be on the engine, moving up and down the ground and waving to all who knew us. After the convent, it was unbelievable, a totally different world. When on holiday we loved to help in any way we could. We would count the takings, nearly all copper because the usual price for a ride was one penny. We would also give the men their "subs". They usually asked for money every dinner time and the balance at the end of the day. The money was counted out in five shillings worth of pennies or two and sixpence worth of halfpennies. There were no copper bags from the bank in those days, so we rolled the money out in pieces of newspaper, quite neat rolls about eight inches long.

The men usually had nicknames. Some of them had been with the family for years. There was one called "Chicken", another "Ginger Tommy", "Wingy Billy", "Swanky Teddy", "Smoky Joe" and "Gavvy Billy" (he looked after the Gavioli organ), and there was "Darkie", who was not a black man by the way. We normally had what we called "a wagon lad". He would fill the water cans, shake the carpets every day, empty the bucket and go any errands.

On the fairground we were always interested in everything connected with the family business. We only occasionally had new tunes on our fairground organ, but what a thrill it was to hear them for the first time: "Roaming in the Gloaming", "She's a Lassie from Lancashire", "My Home in Tennessee" and "Swanee". I remember the first time we heard them and how the whole family came out to listen.

I remember once when we visited a town we had not previously been to. It was a very warm day and mother sat on the caravan steps with the baby in her arms and Janie, May and I clustered round her, talking and laughing. A woman coming off the fairground had with her a little boy aged about five. He was sobbing bitterly. He didn't want to leave the fair and go home, but his mother had no intention of letting him stay. "I've told him, Missus," she said to mother, "He can't stay. If he does, your people will steal him and he'll never see his mammy any more. Isn't that right? You do steal children, don't you?"

"Well," said mother, "I've five beautiful children of my own and I certainly don't want yours or anybody else's and I think you are very silly to frighten your child like that." The woman looked at her in amazement and marched her son off quickly. Mother didn't see the funny side of it at all, as my father did. He said, "My God, it takes me all my time to keep five of them without looking for any more. But I wouldn't swap these for all the tea in China."

We always had a feeling that we were loved and precious to our parents and our family.

Mitchells had been visiting many of the Lancashire towns and fairs for three generations.

The organ in the four abreast Gallopers was also built by Gavioli of Paris. It was the first organ to come to Britain that was operated by cardboard music books. Previous organs had been operated by a pinned barrel, so the variety of tunes had been more limited. The organ still survives in the ownership of Brian Dunsford.

We were known and respected by the townspeople and we of course knew many of them. The fairs we attended were always on hard ground, so that there was no danger of traction engines or trucks sinking, which sometimes happened when a fairground was set up in a park or farmer's field.

Once when we were at Leigh in Lancashire, the showmen there arranged for a char-a-banc to take about twenty four of us to Knutsford in Cheshire. Knutsford Fair was the most beautiful fair I had seen. There were trees and grass everywhere and the showmen had gone to a great deal of trouble to make their equipment look attractive. It was Sunday, so the fair was not open. The May Queen had been crowned the previous day. Quite a number of our relatives were there and we were warmly welcomed by the Sedgwick family. Aunt Harriet and uncle Arthur made us feel at home immediately. They were really my cousin's relations, but we were a close-knit community and they formed part of the family circle. Six of us had arrived without warning but within minutes we were sitting down to a meal which we thoroughly enjoyed. Harriet was a kind and loving person. She had five children, as mother had, but, whereas we had two boys and three girls, she had three boys and two girls. One girl, Prudence, was very fair and the other daughter, Gertie, was dark haired and quite different in appearance.

Sedgwicks had a menagerie. Harriet performed the "butterfly dance" on the front of the menagerie. This free show attracted paying customers into the booth. During the performance Arthur dressed in a red uniform with gold braid, entered the lions' cage and did the lion taming act.

That 1914 holiday! We had been home about a week when war was declared on the 4th August. I was eight years old and my first question was, "What will they call this war in the History books Daddy?" I remember my father pausing before he answered seriously, "I'm afraid it will be the Great European War. A lot of nations will be drawn in before it's over."

The holidays were always bright and enjoyable. No matter how hard I resolved to be, and no matter how much I fought against it, tears would rain down my cheeks as I said goodbye to my parents when I left home for school. My two younger sisters always put me to shame by their stoicism, but my tears seemed independent of my will. It played havoc with resolutions. Disconsolate and inconsolable I always left my dear sweet mother in a load of tears. When we arrived back at school I was astonished to find that the nuns had already heard about the war. The convent was so remote that I could not imagine news coming through.

Uncle Arthur and Aunt Harriet Sedgwick's 'Wild Beast' Menagerie at Leicester in 1909.

LIFE AT THE CONVENT

Back at the convent once more, I would settle down very quickly to my lessons and got quite a lot of pleasure from them. School hours were happy hours. My idea of heaven at the time was a tremendous library filled with more books than I could ever read. I had discovered Dickens, Shakespeare, Sir Walter Scott, Mrs. Henry Wood, Louisa M. Alcock, and Fenimore Cooper. What a mixture!

I also played cards (mostly whist) always for buttons, and there was Ludo, Halina, Snakes and Ladders and even tiddly winks in the winter. In the summer we played cricket, which I thoroughly enjoyed. How it came about I never discovered. It seemed a strange choice for the nuns to have made, but it was played when I went in 1913 and was still a favourite when I left in 1920.

But "Ghosts" was our biggest thrill. Occasionally in the winter the word would go round that a Ghost had been seen in the "Little Yard" and after much prompting and giggling we would see one or two ghostly figures waving their arms and moaning. The doors would be quickly closed. Loud hysterical screams from us would follow and we would rush into the Refectory hiding under the table, chairs or even in the cupboards. Sometimes the ghosts would follow moaning and gesticulating down the passage and then rushing upstairs to the dormitory.

Though we all knew that it was just the bigger girls dressed in sheets playing a practical joke, we always had the fear that it might be ghosts and our hysterical laughter took some time to subside.

We also loved frightening stories and one nun had a stock of these which she would relate to a hushed audience with melodramatic effectiveness. One was a particular favourite. A life size crucifix had been presented to the convent by an unknown donor. This was so beautifully made that it was hung in the convent chapel. One night, one of the nuns was kneeling in front of the crucifix when she saw the eyes move. She did not betray any emotion but continued her prayers, made the sign of the Cross and then left the chapel. Hurrying to the Rev. Mother she told her what had happened. Rev. Mother sent for the police who arrived in time to trap the villain, who was in the act of stealing the gold Sacred Vessels.

Remember we were in the country, the lamps were oil lit and the passages long and shadowy. After such tales we would scuttle fearfully to our beds looking underneath to make sure that no burglar was hiding there.

We spent our Christmas holidays at the convent. It was a busy time for our parents and the nuns made that holiday the highlight of the year. There was always a huge Christmas tree with a present for each child. We would have the gramophone playing in the evening. What a miscellaneous collection of records: "Ave Maria" and "Will You Stop Your Tickling Jock". We would dance and have lemonade and orangeade. On "Holy Innocents' Day" it was a tradition that a Queen, two Princesses and a Court Jester be nominated. They were dressed in suitable clothes for such roles. The "Jester" was the principal of the day, calling on everyone to do and say ridiculous things. The girl chosen would wear motley complete with cap bells and a stick. I remember we all had to pay tribute to the Queen and two Princesses, approaching the throne, solemnly bowing three times and then kissing the hand of the Queen.

The Christmas plays were also a great event and were rehearsed for weeks beforehand. I loved acting and sometimes had two or three parts in a play. Rushing on and off the stage, changing my costume and being in turn a Doctor, a market woman and a sailor within half an hour. The play was produced on three successive evenings and the village people were invited to attend. They nobly supported and applauded us and every play was said to be "even better than the last." During the war, wounded soldiers convalescing in the nearby mansion (Newnham, home of Earl Denbigh) were invited. They were a wonderful audience and full of laughter and cheerfulness. What these scarred heroes really thought of the little girls doing handkerchief dances, scarf drill and enacting very amateurish plays I cannot imagine.

During one play May, always a little nervous at any public exhibition, disgraced the family by starting to giggle. Unfortunately the contagion spread like wildfire and the audience was treated to a display of hysterical laughter which caught everyone on the stage except the pianist who struggled manfully to the end of the song.

On another occasion trouble was caused by the Rev. Mother who was an extremely modest person.

One of the girls taking the part of a penniless orphan had to appear barefooted. As soon as she walked on the stage, Rev. Mother immediately raised her arms in horror and began a series of signals which left us all completely at sea. As she was sat in the front row and visible to the rest of the audience, they became extremely restless and the play finished in some confusion. But penniless or not, the next evening saw the bare legged orphan bare legged no more, but clad in very adequate and concealing black woollen stockings.

Once the pianist's dark frizzy hair caught fire. Candles had been lit on either side of her in the holders specially made for this purpose. Before she could realise what had happened, a wounded soldier was on the spot, the fire had been extinguished and the play went on without a commotion.

One of the great pleasures of my life was the walk to the church, about a mile distant, for Benediction on Sunday winter evenings. During the 1914-18 war searchlights would occasionally stab the sky and move in geometrical patterns.

The tree lined avenue was like a stage backcloth, the road gently sweeping up the hill, with the dark outline of hedges and sheep nearby. Every hundred yards had its landmark. The gate with "private road" leading to the estate. "Peg's Hole" was next with its beech nuts and sandy soil

contrasting with the surrounding green. This was followed by the hilly avenue, and then the gates which marked the beginning of the grounds of Newnham. These gates could be automatically opened by cars being driven over the iron hoops some distance away and then closed in the same manner. Next came the view of cypress and firtrees with the lovely wilderness. This was a jungle like garden overgrown with tall weeds and wild flowers through which we sometimes walked. Then came the stately house of the Fieldings with the church built on. This spacious church built by a fervent and optimistic Catholic Earl with its many pews sparsely occupied by a handful of villagers. The Fielding family seated on one side, while the younger convent children occupied the other. The older girls were moved to the choir, as soon as they were able to read music, whether they had been blessed with a good singing voice or not. I was one of the "have nots" in common with all my family but this did not prevent me from singing a husky solo on occasions. This happened at the wedding of Lady Clare and Group Captain Smyth-Pigott in December 1919. I remember Earl Denbigh asking to meet the soloist afterwards. He was very courteous and thanked me. I have often laughed since and wondered what was really in his mind.

The nuns thought a lot of the family at the Hall, and we knew much of their history; of the tragic

A War Department Foden steam wagon similar to the one driven in France by Jack Mitchell during the First War.

Uncle Willie's Scenic Motors with a compliment of soldiers. It must have been photographed early in the war before he was forced to close down due to lack of staff and stringent regulations imposed under the Defence of the Realm Act.

death of Monsignor Basil who died "shooting the rapids", of Lady Winefride who had been attacked and crippled by one of her father's swans. Later still we were to pray for the two gallant sons who lost their lives during the war. Hugh (a Lieutenant Commander) at Jutland on 31st May 1916, and Henry who died of his wounds at Flanders in October 1917. They were soon followed by their mother, and I remember that dark stormy December Sunday evening after her death, when someone tiptoed gently to her husband in chapel to whisper of the birth of a grandchild. Death and birth so close at hand.

The four years of war passed like a long drawn nightmare. Green shades had to be fixed on all fairground lamps. Staff were hard to get and air raids became commonplace. Prices soared and butter was 5 shillings a lb., bacon likewise. People whom I had always known to be poor suddenly blossomed forth as the "new rich". Factory girls bought fur coats for the first time in their lives. The cry seemed to be not, "How much is it?" but "Can you get it?" Money in Lancashire flowed freely, but it wasn't easy money by any means on the fairground. Uncle Willie gave up the unequal struggle and closed down his roundabout. Uncle

Bennie turned down by the Medical Board carried on against great odds. My father, strong, virile, little Hercules, was assessed grade four and went to Sheffield to work on munitions. My dear mother, surprisingly intuitive on this occasion rejoiced that he had been spared. She carried on with the help of my grandfather (now nearing eighty) despite tremendous difficulties.

During the war my cousin Jack Mitchell was gassed whilst serving with the army in France. He was later captured by the Germans while driving a steam wagon near Chemin des Dames, and remained a prisoner until the end of the war. When he returned home he was in poor health. The family did whatever they could to improve his health but it was sometime before he was himself again. His breathing and chest never fully recovered from the effect of the mustard gas. One of Jack's favourite expressions was " nicht arbeit, nicht essen" (no work, no food), which was an expression he learned to his cost during his captivity.

The peace of 1918. Uncle Bennie, victim of the dreadful Spanish Flu had been buried in Preston cemetery in July. Less than twelve months later the Medical Board's decision was vindicated when my father died of cancer in June 1919.

SOUTHPORT

At 14 my future became a worry. What was I to do? I had learned all that the convent school could teach me. My mother thought, and suggested, a Commercial Training College and boarding school. One in Southport was eventually chosen. It was an expensive school, but my mother did not hesitate. To her and to me it seemed ideal, and so at 15 I went to Oakworth.

Oakworth was a secretarial school for gentlewomen. There was a certain amount of snobbish comment at the time. My mother thought it better not to disclose that we came from the fairground and she told me on no account to mention this. She really believed that it might harm my chances at the school and that the Headmaster himself might raise objections on account of the other parents' attitude.

My position was perfectly awful. I had to be constantly on my guard and not say that I lived in a caravan. As every holiday I returned to a different town it became more and more difficult. However if the parents were snobs, the other girls were not, and they must have sensed that I did not wish to be questioned and so, strangely enough after a while my "skeleton in the cupboard" became smaller and smaller, and even when I left, my home life was never mentioned.

I was a demon for work but was terribly homesick. I was very conscious of the fact that I was different from the other pupils, many of whom came from well to do families of professional and businessmen. I was also younger than the others; their ages ranged from 17 upwards, and for the first time I was completely "at sea". I took refuge in my studies. Typewriting seemed to come easily to me. My fingers skipped easily and rapidly on the keyboard.

Before I had been typing for a month I had caught up to the girls who had been there for two. One of them asked me how many pages of each exercise I had done. "Twenty of each," I answered. "Just as the instructions say." "Ah," she said, "It really means twenty both sides, forty in all." I took her at her word and did forty and still caught up with the others although they were only doing twenty.

Whenever I had any spare time, I would go to a typewriter and do exercises and exercises. I typed the alphabet backwards and forwards 21,000 times.

When I got to the end of a textbook, I started at the beginning again and went through it three times. I knew what I wanted and drove myself desperately.

Luckily I had a wonderful teacher, Mr. Frank Wood who was also the principal of the College. He realised my possibilities as a speed typist during my first term as he had previously trained one "Champion Typist of Europe". He fired me with his own enthusiasm, and I too had that end in view.

During this time at "Oakworth" he told me that I showed promise of carrying off that honour too. His method of training was unusual. He would ask me to type exercises or extracts from the newspaper, starting with a stop-watch, and then, while I was concentrating hard and striving to attain the highest speed my fingers were capable of doing, he would throw a metal typewriter cover over my head with tremendous gusto, the deafening noise resulting when it reached the floor being nerve-racking, to say the least. This would be followed by other objects, and he would ring a bell, shout and generally do his best to distract me while I was typing a particularly difficult piece. I soon got accustomed to these poltergeist ways and, being only 15, looked upon it as a game and one in which I was determined to score. At the convent I had been a source of amusement to the other girls. When engrossed in a book I would read oblivious of the noise around me and many a time the night bell had gone and I had to be literally shaken out of a "brown study" to come to earth. Now I concentrated on my typewriter in the same way, and oblivious of flying covers and clanging bells, stuck solidly to the "copy" with which I was dealing and ignored the rumpus.

Mr Wood delighted in my work and helped and encouraged me unceasingly. He dictated to me direct, so that I could get accustomed to typing "verbatim" reports. He gave me finger exercises to strengthen the muscles and advised rubbing my hands with olive oil before every examination. We both took it all very seriously, but when I went home for the holidays my mother and family had no idea what it was all about. I don't think mother had ever seen a typewriter operated. It was something she had heard about as an instrument of a "refined" occupation and she was more than delighted to receive glowing reports from Southport.

On one of my half term holidays from

Southport, I remember coming home to Bury. Our caravan had a vertical pole, about ten foot long, very near to it. The bottom of the pole was driven into the ground and there was a wire which went from the pole into our living wagon. When I went up the steps I was annoyed to find that instead of the usual greeting, I was frowned at and "shushed" in no uncertain manner by Billy and Tom.

They both had earphones on, or at least they had one earphone each. (They had dismantled a set and detached one earphone, to enable two people to listen.) Tom took his off, "Come on" he said excitedly, "Listen, all the way from Manchester. Someone's playing on a piano. Manchester's ten miles away. Isn't it wonderful?" My first introduction to wireless. It was marvellous but very anti-social with earphones. I spent that weekend listening, "shushing" and being "shushed".

My brother's friend, Bob Green (later to become my husband) not only had one of the new wireless sets but had taken out a licence which allowed him to transmit radio signals as well. That weekend was a thrilling one, March 1921 or 1922.

In 1922 when I was sixteen I was asked to go to Paris, with three other girls to compete for the International Trophy. Mother willingly gave her consent and saw that I had everything necessary for the adventure. Mr. Wood, three other girls, myself and a chaperone set forth on this momentous journey, first of all to London, where we were entertained by an American Typewriter Company. We left Victoria the next day by first class reserved coach for Dover, a large sitting room with armchairs and tables luxuriously fitted was at our disposal. The stationmaster, complete with top hat, saw us off at Victoria. At Dover the boat train awaited us and several hundred other passengers. A howling gale with grey seas, sullen skies and icy winds made the crossing sheer torture.

The top deck was roped off, as it was considered unsafe for anyone to use. The sea swirled over the side of the lower deck four inches deep, cascading from one side of the boat to the other as it rocked with the force of the waves. I have crossed the

The Oakworth College team of high speed typists, myself on the front row second from the right.

59

A French publicity shot of me at the keyboard of a Royal Typewriter, which was used in the International Typing Competition of 1922. I tied with the champion from the previous year at 3499 strokes in five minutes, and was awarded second prize.

Channel many times since but this was my worst crossing. Calais at last and four shivering, seasick girls set foot on French soil to be confronted by blue smocked dark haired Frenchmen, strong as bulls, carrying four or five times the amount of luggage strapped around their torso that an English porter would have lifted. And within five minutes of boarding the warm, cosy French train and the serving of hot drinks, the discomforts of the trip were forgotten and it became exciting, interesting and thrilling once more.

I have forgotten the restaurants we visited and the food we had. I know it seemed strange and not altogether palatable that first visit. But I shall never forget my first typewriting contest, and the tense excited atmosphere when we entered the Salle de Concours. Fifty typewriters on fifty desks with a flag flying beside each one indicating the nationalities of the competitor: German, Turkish, French, Belgian, Italian etc. The contest itself consisted in those days of a five minute test of memorised text.

The clicking of the keys, the ringing of the carriage bells, the inserting of the paper as each contestant got to work. Then a whistle blew and the silence that followed could be felt. The President de Concours read out the rules in French, which were then translated. Desks were cleared of everything save typewriters. Fresh stamped paper was issued and inserted in every machine. Are you ready? And the whistle blew and we were off, oblivious to the world. Poor Mr. Wood standing close by, with eyes glued on his "team" must have gone through a gruelling five minutes. I was in a world of my own, fingers flying, keys responding, carriage tripping backwards and forwards with a rhythm known and expected. I wasn't in France or even out of England, I was doing the work I was accustomed to at school and oblivious of everyone until the whistle went again. The quiet that followed was frightening in the tremendous relief that it brought. Papers signed, papers collected.

Mr Wood came and patted me on the shoulder. "You've done wonderfully well," he said. "I don't know how you've gone on for errors but you've beaten everybody here for speed." I had tied with the Champion, Miss Woodward. When the results were made known there was bewilderment. That a schoolgirl could come over and outclass people older and with many more years experience seemed incredible. It was decided to award the cup to Miss Woodward who was already the holder. For future competitions it was decided to make the contest a twenty minute test, copying from a newspaper of the day.

Everyone was loud in their praise and Mr. Wood was afraid it might go to my head, but there was no risk of that. I tasted champagne, and like most youngsters thought it merely "pop". I enjoyed the fuss and had a really wonderful time that November in 1922, so many years ago. I was small and looked younger than sixteen and became quite a sensation. My photograph was in the newspapers, (English, French and even American), and I realised that my hard work had "lifted me out of the rut".

I had created a problem. I was acknowledged as the fastest typist in Europe. What was I to do? Stay at Oakworth? Mr. Wood firmly recommended it

The gold pin and badge which were awarded to me at the 2nd International Typing Competition in Paris in 1922.

and I realised he was right. "Stay at Oakworth" mother echoed.

So stay at Southport I did. I realised that I was still not good enough, and so for the next two years I continued my commercial training, French, book-keeping and shorthand, but always typewriting whenever I had a chance and always with the European Typing Championship in mind. At this time England was in the doldrums. Unemployment was the order of the day and skilled and energetic men anxious and willing for work were idle. I determined that my skill would be such that I should never be in that position. My father was dead, our travelling business was losing money. I felt that in me lay the hope of keeping the family in reasonable circumstances. I worked hard and won the European Typewriting Championship in 1924. What next?

(Left) The photograph which was used on my passport in 1923.

61

COLLEGE HOLIDAYS

When I was eighteen and at home on holiday, I was told that my cousin Lizzie was expecting her second baby. Her sister Lucy, who was also eighteen and a bit of a comedian, came into the caravan in great excitement.

"Our Lizzie has had twins, auntie," she announced. Mother started to laugh. We all knew Lucy and her funny sense of humour. "Lucy, don't make jokes like that," said mother. "But it's true, auntie, I've just seen her. They are two little girls." Mother was obviously upset. All the family knew that Lizzie wanted a little boy. "How is Lizzie?" she asked. "Oh, she's fine. When I left her, she had a big plateful of meat and potato pie and all the boys, our Billy and Bennie and your Billy, were with her and they were laughing and talking and looking at the babies."

Mother was astonished. She had always had trouble when she had her children and she was anxious in case Lizzie was not being looked after properly. Lizzie had gone to a friend's house in Heywood to have her babies. Meat and potato pie was not mother's idea of feeding an invalid. Gruel, soup and warm milk would have been given to Lizzie for the first few days, so mother went down immediately to see the twins and Lizzie. Sure enough there were quite a number of young folks in the room, laughing and happy. Lizzie herself seemed as fit as a fiddle, but mother thought she should have quiet and rest for the next few hours. Her face lit up as she held the babies for the first time.

They were identical twins and this was confirmed as they grew older. When they were about four years old, they went with their mother to a house in Tyldesley and, while the grown-ups were talking, the twins were chasing each other from the front door into the kitchen and out of the back door, round the house and through the front door again. The little girl of the house watched them in amazement and sidled up to her mother and whispered, "How many of them are there?" To her it seemed that a continuous stream of identical little girls were in and out all the time.

When the babies were a few days old, Lizzie asked her husband to arrange for their baptism or christening, as it was more generally known. My brother Billy and I were to be godparents to Nona and cousin Billy and my sister Janie were to be godparents to the other twin Edith. The service was to take place on Sunday afternoon. There was a carpet of snow on the ground when we arrived. A service was taking place, so we had to wait for about half an hour before we could go in. This was too good an opportunity for the boys to miss and, while Janie and I nursed the babies, the boys threw snowballs and had fun and games on the field outside.

When we eventually went into the church, the boys still covered in snow, the priest took all four godparents to one side, explained the procedure to us and asked for our names and addresses so that he could enter them in the Church records. This however caused the priest to be rather confused. We had no house at the time, as we were permanent caravan dwellers, but grandfather had arranged with his solicitor to use his address for all correspondence.

Billy and cousin Billy were both named William Mitchell, both about the same age and gave the same address, so, as the priest explained, it would appear in the records that the same person had acted as godfather to both the twins. However, our boys had no middle name, so the priest eventually registered them as godparents. Lizzie had told them to give half-a-crown each to the priest after the christening and I could see my brother Billy and cousin Billy kissing their half-crowns goodbye before they handed them over. Fred, the twin's father, was most indignant and promised to pay them back when they got home.

During the Depression the roundabouts on the fair took very little money because there was so much unemployment in the mining and cotton towns. It was heart rending to see the miners squatting on the pavement edge, talking to each other, just passing the time away. They reminded me of flocks of birds on telegraph wires.

The Slump made for reduced earnings and, if the weather was bad, it was really not worth opening the adult roundabouts. If it was dull, our boys prayed for rain, so that they could go to "the pictures". When it was really threatening, one of the boys would climb onto grandad's caravan roof and the other two would hand up the big cans of water every showman had. They would pour water onto the roof top, down the windows and the front door, trying to convince grandfather that it would be wiser not to open as no one would want to come on, in such heavy rain. If they succeeded, they would go to the local cinema to see a cowboy film. Despite his poor sight grandfather was not always convinced. If the fair did not open, there was no prospect of taking any money. He would also have to give his grandchildren spending money.

An alternative for fairground youngsters was the drink shop, a local soft drink and ice cream parlour.

In those days there was at least one in every town. This was a real magnet for showland children. They sat on high stools near the bar or on chairs round small tables, laughing and talking, telling each other of the different fairs they had visited. If any of the local children visited the group, they were usually welcomed and many friendships were formed that way.

My Brother Tom

Uncle Bennie's daughter Lizzie, my cousin, and her husband Fred Carter with their daughter Joan. In the doorway of the wagon on the right is her brother Billy Mitchell.

PARIS

My teacher, Mr. Wood, had heard from a French typewriting firm (MAP owned by F.N.) asking if I would consider a 12 month contract in Paris as demonstrator of their machine. This sounded attractive to me and I persuaded my mother to let me accept the offer. But she insisted that my sister Janie was to go with me as my companion. I was 18, Janie was around 16 and like two babes in the wood we crossed the Channel and travelled to Paris. When we arrived no one met us and our first necessity was to find an hotel, where I booked a room for the night. What complete innocents we were. Neither of us could speak more than a few sentences in French, neither of us had any idea of the character and behaviour of the people around us, but with supreme confidence in ourselves and with our Guardian Angels as protectors we managed beautifully.

The next morning we took a taxi to the factory at St.Dennis on the outskirts of Paris. I met the Managing Director who spoke perfect English and who was married to an English woman. I felt once more that I was among friends. They accepted Janie without surprise and promptly put her on the payroll. She gained valuable secretarial experience and worked from my office. After two years Janie returned to England to help mother on the fairground and my younger sister May became my companion and also had a similar job to Janie.

How kind they were to me and how I got to know and love the French people and France during the four years I was there. Our Director arranged for us to stay with an English family in St. Ouen, Mr. and Mrs Yapp and their two children, Doris and May. We were reasonably happy there until the children caught scarlet fever and we had to move. This time we went to a French family. Madame Joffre was a widow with a daughter of 30 and a son of 22. Her three other sons had been killed in the 1914 war. Suzanne worked in the accounts department in the office where I worked. Felix was a sculptor, a student of the Ecole des Beaux Arts. (who later won the Prix de Rome in 1928, and died in 1982). Through him we became acquainted with other young artists, painters, writers and sculptors. Some were Parisian, others from the provinces and a few from Algeria. Janie and I listened wide eyed and fascinated when they talked of their student

My sister Janie, cousin Lizzie and May Sedgwick on Mitchell's Four Abreast Gallopers. To the left is the steam centre engine which drove the ride.

life. They were young, lively and happy go lucky. They talked seriously of politics and the inevitability of Communism in Russia. They discussed writers, Shaw, Rousseau, Byron, and Moliere. They introduced us to an entirely brave new world. They laughed and sometimes teased us but they never told a blue joke or used a "smutty" word.

We visited their studios, and made the rounds of the museums and picture galleries following their good advice. I remember one evening when we were sitting down to an evening meal, Roger Pratt (another 25 year old sculptor and Felix's bosom pal) was with us. On the little cat's whisker wireless set we had heard that Lindberg was expected. "Faney" Pratt was saying, "a chap our age, all alone, in that small plane, over the vast Atlantic Ocean. Quel type!" Well Lindberg did make it and Paris went crazy. I can picture him now, tall, lean, shy, fair and curly haired and very tired after his long nerve racking flight. Poor boy, what tragedy lay ahead with the kidnapping and death of his baby son in 1932.

Another of our friends was a clerk named Marthe. She was as sturdy as an English oak. In a country where the petite, chic and essentially feminine woman was admired, Marthe was somewhat of a freak and yet she attracted men as surely as pollen does the bees. She was of Polish descent, with finely chiselled strong features, beautiful large grey eyes set with dark thick lashes and with bright chestnut hair. Her body was heavily built, and her legs and arms were thick and shapeless. "Taille avec une hache" I have heard her described as, on more than one occasion, and it was said in an uncomplimentary fashion. But Marthe laughed at such criticism; in fact she agreed with it, and rather enjoyed her heavy frame

She was earning a bare pittance when I first met her, and being without relatives, had to live in furnished rooms. She had to clothe and feed herself on the equivalent of a pre-war 25 shillings a week. But she was gay, so gay, and her vivid clothes made and designed by herself would have graced Isadora Duncan. She occasionally sported a lavender cloak and "papillon, papillon" the errand boys yelled after her when the wind caught it and carried her along like an exotic butterfly. Marthe would laugh back to the cheeky youngsters.

Once she invited me to tea. Her room was a small one in a new high apartment house near the

My sister May. After Janie had worked for two years in Paris my mother decided it was my younger sisters turn. May came and lived with me and also had a job at the MAP factory.

Flea Market. The furniture was cheap and tawdry but bright. The high new building was narrow and incongruous in that particular part of Paris, where old and ramshackle decrepit wooden structures were numerous. From Marthe's window I could see a typical shack, in which a family lived and flourished. In their tiny ten foot yard a solitary cow gazed forlornly at its weird surroundings occasionally "mooing" to its unheeding human neighbours. Marthe loved animals and would occasionally talk gently back to the beast from her fifth storey perch.

Marthe moved house frequently and I once spent the night with her in a studio loaned to her by a painter who had gone to his parents' house for the summer holiday. The creaking stairs led to a kind of balcony alcove which contained a bed, and the ground floor studio served as living room and wash room. I think the studio had been built originally as a coach house. The huge wooden doors gave me that impression and the bedroom was very reminiscent of a hay loft. The painter had left proofs of his work everywhere and what peculiar masterpieces they were. Marthe proudly showed me one which was of two nude hefty women. The picture could be turned upright or upside down and was exactly the same in either position. I found it repulsive and in questionable taste, but Marthe spoke as an accomplished critic and pronounced it as a fine study.

Coming home one day on the Underground she found her shoes were pinching her. Without more ado she took them off and walked through Paris in her stocking feet. She usually went about bare headed, but on one occasion she was wearing a rather expensive hat and when it began to rain, off came the hat, and under her cloak it went. "My hair

will wash and costs nothing" she said, "but my hat will be ruined if it should get wet." She treated everyone as equal: directors, managers, errand boys and the occasional gypsy we met in the suburbs. Marthe was a friend of all the world, but she was happiest among the young artists of L'Ecole des Beaux Arts, who loved her. "C'est une bonne fille" they used to say with admiration and respect. Surely no one could deserve higher praise than that accorded by those generous and warm hearted young men.

Dear sweet Marthe. What I wonder did the Pole hating Gestapo ridden Nazi occupied France do to her? May she have eluded and outwitted them all. I stayed four years in France and loved every week of it. I visited every city of importance and found Marseilles the peach of them all. What a wonderful thrill to see the blue Mediterranean and ride along the Corniche. My heart leapt at the sight of a palm tree, symbol of the East and the Biblical tales of old. The colonial fezzed and turbaned men on the Cannebriere caught my imagination. The ships laden with fish in the harbour with birds swooping to devour an easy meal. The Chateau and prison of the "Count of Monte Cristo", the olive trees, the beaded curtains and the red tiled polished floors. The fish and saffron soup lightly spiced and appetising, a soup the colour of which I never imagined existed, and the warm sun bathing everything in lavish colour. The Black Virgin in the church on the mountain smiled as enigmatically as the Mona Lisa, while black, white, brown and yellow pilgrims gazed at her in curiosity or devotion. While the models of ships hung around the church, mute pleas for protection to the great almighty against the elements. What a lovely City, the beginning and end, I thought, of Western civilisation.

And Lille, the Manchester of France where I was entertained like a princess. Amiens, the Venice of France, with it's rivulets and streams running through narrow streets and where I ate strawberries as big as any I had enjoyed in England. Asnières sur Seine where I was presented with a gold medal and a certificate saying I was the speediest typist in the world, and Lyons where I visited the famous "Doire de Lyons" and drank a concoction of chocolate and coffee which I have never heard of since. And that wonderful restaurant, La Mere Fillioux, where a roast chicken was served at every table for the diner to carve himself. The poor waiter

had to collect the uneaten food. The kitchen was open to all and sundry to inspect, though inspection was not part of my programme. I enjoyed every mouthful of every delicious meal and was content to accept and enjoy the food so beautifully cooked and served.

I learned to appreciate good wines and knew a Barsac from a Sauterne or a Graves. I was soon to recognise a good Beaune, to order Vin du Pays and to enjoy the cheeses of the different Provinces in which I travelled. Goats cheese I never really found appetising but Brie and Camembert were dreams of delight which haunted me through the drought of the war years. How I longed for some crusty rolls and that creamy cheese and visions of past meals blunted my humour during that dreary period.

Lovely France and kindly France. How good everyone was to me and what a delight to discover the foreign charm of life outside Great Britain. While my stomach warmed to the good food my mind warmed to the people, the artists I met, the office staff I mixed with, and the audiences I demonstrated to. To me La Belle France was indeed "La Belle France" and to her I owe a debt of gratitude. Indeed may my children love her as I do. However I left France in 1928. Mother had given up travelling from fair to fair and had rented a flat in Paddington, London. I had been offered a good job in the Capital by an American firm.

The Challenge Cup which became mine after I had won the competition in three successive years.

LONDON

I started work with L.C.Smith and Corona in August 1928, and remained with them until the spring of 1937 when I was married and left their employ to return to the fairground with my husband Robert Green.

In the years I worked in London I saw much of the pageantry there. The Lord Mayor's show and the opening of Parliament were annual events guaranteed to make the heart of any citizen beat faster, and I was no exception. Rather my lively imagination added further colour to these ceremonies and I revelled in their traditions and magnificence. I became a sightseer and a rubber neck. Because of my position I saw much not usually seen by the person in the street. On one occasion when Mr. Ramsay Mc.Donald was Prime Minister I visited Number 10 Downing Street and met his secretary, a cheery and efficient lady who had recently visited the U.S.. She had seen the factory at Syracuse, which manufactured the typewriter I used.

My European Championship cup which was displayed in the L.C.Smith window in the photograph below.

L.C.Smith & Corona's London office with a poster in the window advertising that I was demonstrating on an L.C.Smith Ball Bearing Typewriter. One of my cups is also in the window.

I was struck by the shape of the basket chair occupied by the doorman, like a cradle turned upright and reminiscent of the beach chair I had seen at the seaside resort of Scheveningen, near The Hague in Holland. Number 10 Downing Street was unpretentious and Victorian. I was thrilled to think of the momentous decisions which had been made there and of the people who had made them.

In Paris I had visited the Senate House and demonstrated at the Chamber of Deputies. I had typed in French, English and Esperanto. I had been warmly praised and cordially treated but in England I was "at home" and very conscious of the distinction of even entering Number 10. But the visit to Downing Street, wonderful though it was, paled into insignificance when I learned I was to go to St. James' Palace in order to collect and bring back a speech in French which was to be typed by me for H.R.H. the Prince of Wales. He was due to visit Paris a week later. I remember the first time I visited the Palace, the Boy Scout at the door who led me to Mr. Carter, the Comptroller of the Prince's household, who in turn led me to Sir Godfrey Thomas, the Prince's Private Secretary. I took back the rough manuscript of the speech, typed it at the office and returned it to St. James'. I remember the Duke of Kent's chauffeur in black alpine coat waiting for his master at the door. The youngest Royal Prince had at the time been forbidden to drive as he had been caught speeding down the Mall and his family were anxious for his own and the public's safety.

I visited the Admiralty too and met distinguished Civil Servants. The fruits of my endeavours tasted sweet indeed. The B.B.C. were doing a series of "In Town Tonight", and when I was in Chelmsford I received a telephone message asking me to visit Savoy Hill. There was no time to tell my mother and family. That night they were astonished to hear me being introduced over the air and to hear what they called my "machine gun" rattling on the wireless.

I also had requests from Gaumont and Pathé News. They made newsreels which were exhibited around the world. Friends and relatives later commented about seeing me on these newsreels

I met the Duke of York (later King George VI) at an Exhibition at Northampton. He congratulated me on my typewriting and asked me where I came from. This was so unexpected a question that I found myself replying Manchester, city of my birth but one in which I had not lived since I was three weeks old. How I admired the Duke for his great courage. At the time he had an impediment in his speech so acute that occasionally his jaw appeared to be almost locked. It seemed impossible for him to talk, but in spite of this and in front of a crowd of thousands he made a long speech opening the Trades Exhibition. To me it was an inspiration. I too in my small way had to make speeches, at schools and at exhibitions, and I felt never again would I be afraid to face the public. I felt humble at H.R.H.'s courage.

I saw King George V open India House in Aldwych. He looked frail, ill and infinitely weary, while Queen Mary, upright and regal at his side, smiled and bowed. When his death came the country mourned wholeheartedly, acknowledging his great reign and worth. Along with thousands I queued to pay my final homage at Westminster Hall, and an awe inspiring sight it was. The Royal coffin draped by the Royal Standard in gold and

A publicity photograph of me operating a portable typewriter in Richmond Park. The Austin 7 and the small dog were described as being mine. I did own an Austin 7, but it was not as good as this one, and our family dog was a mongrel.

A post card of the aeroplane "Hengist" in which I flew from Croydon to Paris to take part in a Competition in the early 1930's. At the time the Heracles class of Imperial Airways 'Liners' were the largest civil aeroplanes in the world, and the first with four engines. There was a crew of four, and seats for 38 passengers. The cruising speed was 100 m.p.h.

scarlet, was mounted by the orb and crown. A solitary white, wreath once magnificent but wilted and infinitely lovely, proclaimed his widow's love to the world.

The richly uniformed guards stood at each corner of the catafalque in the bare splendour of the historic hall, where King Charles I had been condemned to die. Never shall I forget that truly wonderful sight of the hushed people passing the dead monarch in this ancient hall. A hall which had seen so many generations of monarchy, so many generations of our people in splendour and in sorrow. I was also present at the funeral on the 20th

January 1936 and saw the four sons, Edward VIII, the Duke of York, the Duke of Gloucester and the Duke of Kent walking behind the coffin. There was Royalty from many lands following in their wake. I remember the little final human touch of George and Gerald Lascelles, the two young sons of Princess Mary the Princess Royal, who were so interested in the crowd, leaning out of the window of the carriage, with the younger one, Gerald, energetically gyrating his head for all the world to see. Taut and strung up as we were by the solemnity of the Royal death, we were forced to smile at his boyish behaviour.

Some of the medals which were awarded to me over the years after winning European typing championships.

70

POSTSCRIPT BY THE EDITOR

My mother did not write any more about her life. She did however write some poetry and one of her poems is printed on the inside front cover.

My parents travelled and operated a caterpillar roundabout attending fairs up and down the country. They had a happy marriage. My brother Peter was born in 1939 shortly after war was declared. I was born in 1944. Mum put as much effort into being a good mother and wife as she had in her career as a champion typist. She eventually sold her house in Southall, London.

In 1968 dad purchased an amusement arcade in Morecambe. Mum and dad soon settled there. Later in the same year Peter was married and went into business with his brother in law in Bolton. By 1972 dad had wound up his Morecambe business and retired. He came out regularly to assist me in running our long established travelling business.

Mother and father enjoyed life in Morecambe, and their house there was a comfortable one. Mum died in 1984 age 78, and dad in 1990 age 88.

Older brother Billy left the business at the end of 1928, and had a varied life. He and his wife Dorothy raised a large family. Billy died in 1974 age 71. Younger sister May had a contented married life and died in 1983 age 72. Sister Janie also found a good husband and lived longest. She died in 2002 age 93. Further details of the family, their children etc. can be found on the family trees on the next pages. I have tried to ensure that everyone is mentioned somewhere in the text but there is a limit.

My parents at Nice in 1951

I thought that as this would be the only book on Mitchells there should be details on all their rides and transport. Kevin Scrivens has very willingly drawn up the details on the following pages. It is surprising to note that Mitchells never owned a Bioscope show.

TOMMY GREEN.

MITCHELLS' RIDES by Kevin Scrivens

George Greens traction centre engine hauling the eight boats from his Sea on Land and an early living wagon.The large road wheels on the boat trucks ran on a circular wooden tramway around the centre engine when the ride was built up. Gearing was connected which rolled the boats from side to side as well as rocking them backwards and forwards.

1881 Sea on Land No.1.

In January 1881 William Mitchell took delivery of what is thought to have been his first steam driven ride, a Sea-on-Land, which was new at Preston Christmas Fair. The ride was built by Savages of Kings Lynn, but driven by a McLaren traction centre engine number 95 built in Leeds. The engine hauled the loads of the ride on the road, and at the fairground the ride was built up around it. To disguise the tall chimney in the centre of the ride it was enclosed by a wooden replica of a lighthouse. This structure was fitted with a gallery near the top where a small band could play to entertain the riders.

1882 Sea on Land No.2.

By October 1882 Mitchell's second Sea on Land made its appearance. This was an almost identical Savage built machine which was new for Hill Bros. of Bristol in February 1881. This ride also had a McLaren traction centre engine, number 100. The rides were known by the public as 'dry land sailors' in those days.

George Twigdon's Sea on Land was built in 1884 for Murphys. It was almost identical to the two Mitchell rides.

1887 Platform Galloper No.1.

This Savage built ride was new in 1887, centre engine number 401. It was reported to be new for Rochdale Wakes Fair that year. In 1894 it was fitted with the top from one of Mitchell's Switchback Galloper rides. In February 1910 it was advertised in the Worlds Fair: *"For sale a set of 4-abreast Savage make flat platform galloping cockerels consisting of 12 sections with two spinners, carved and gilded, New set of trams, Rounding boards, cornice and droppers. Top centre drum and inside droppers, also Gavioli organ and centre engine. Also electric light engine with copper firebox, equal to new, Greens make. New dynamo. 32 Arc 110 volt. Also 14 Excello arc lamps, trucks to carry everything concerning machine, everything ready for taking money, can be made into a set of Porkers if required as we have the pigs to fit this machine. Will sell cheap to immediate customer, or will exchange for another kind of roundabout. Reason for selling we have two machines of one kind. Cash terms to responsible parties, Apply William Mitchell and Sons, 53 Hindhill Street, Heywood."*

1890 Switchback Galloper No.1.

Also known as Mountain Ponies, this ride was new at Stockport on May 1st 1890. It was almost certainly the centre of one of the Sea on Land rides rebuilt by Savages into a new machine.

1891 Switchback Galloper No.2.

In 1891 Savages built another set of Mountain Ponies for William Mitchell and Sons. Drawings describe the ride as a four abreast, with the inside horse mounted on an outrigger. This ride is thought to have been new with Savage centre engine No.517. A report of Tyldesley Bongs Fair 1892 records one of Mitchell's "Mountain Switchback Galloping Horses" being present, fitted with a "Military Band, equal to a band of 50 performers, which cost £1,500".

Oldham Wakes 1905. William Mitchell's four abreast platform Ostriches and Cockerels to the left of the photograph. To the right are Mitchell's Steam Yachts, in front of which is Mitchell's portable electric light engine which was made by Greens of Leeds. This photograph shows another part of the fair seen on page 22.

(Above). The Switchback Galloper was patented by George Green in 1889. This very elaborate version was travelled by Greens themselves. The sections of horses were fitted with gearing beneath the platforms which made the horses rock backwards and forwards at the ride revolved. Mitchell's had two machines of this type.

(Left) A Razzle Dazzle of the type travelled by William Mitchell in the 1890's.

Stockport Fair in the 1890's. On the extreme right is a spinning top Switchback Galloper thought to be William Mitchells. The line of machines from left to right comprise two steam driven sets of Dobby Horses, a Platform Galloper and a Tunnel Railway. Behind the row of rides is a fixed dip Razzle Dazzle, thought to be William Mitchells.

A note on a Savage works drawing dated November 1894 records "Mitchell Switchback Galloper. Standing top altered to large revolving top for Ostriches". The Ostriches were the No.1 Platform Galloper. A new top must have been made for the Switchback Galloper, as a report of Gorton Wakes fair in 1898 records the presence of Mitchell and Son's 2 sets of Mountain Ponies and Platform Ostriches amongst the other rides.

1896 Razzle Dazzle.

The first known Razzle Dazzle was built for J. Howarth of Hollinwood in 1887, soon followed by one for Tom Hurst of Clifton. The third was for George Green of Preston in 1888. By 1890 William Parker of Bury had invented a dipping machine, which sounds somewhat crude, having the circular motion provided by a necessarily strong man turning something similar to a ships wheel perched above the top suspension ring, and the dips provided by men beneath the platform pulling on ropes, which also helped with the circular motion.

This was advertised in the 'Era' in November 1896: *A bargain to immediate purchaser. We are giving up travelling. Parkers improved patent steam ship Razzle Dazzle, 40 foot diameter, seats 100 passengers. New organ and engine, and three trucks. Also flying ship illusion, and one truck. For the lot £250. Apply Parkers, Tent Maker, Bury, Lancs.* This was sold to William Mitchell and travelled for several years.

1896 Galloper.

Little is known about this ride which was advertised for sale in the "Era" newspaper in 1896 as follows *"Wanted to sell very very cheap, set of steam rocking horses (36 horses). Easily allotted to any motion, with platform and double row of steps, Gavioli organ, 90 keys, large and small drum, three figures, and cymbals. 5 loads all in first class order. Apply Mr William Mitchell 53, Hindhill Street, Heywood."* This could be the machine regarding which an action was brought against William Mitchell by Savages for infringement of their patent for the platform slide, although the case was not heard until 1900. The case was dismissed on the grounds that the idea was not patentable.

1900 Steam Yachts.

This ride was built in 1895 by William Cartwright, the inventor and patentee. It was the fourth set of Yachts built by him, and the second with horizontal cylinders on the centre engine, an improvement on his previous design. The ride travelled in the Midlands and Lancashire, and opened alongside Mitchell's rides. At the end of 1900 it was sold to William Mitchell. It was redecorated, and the boats named after two of the racing yachts in the Americas Cup races "Shamrock" (Sir Thomas Lipton's challenge yacht which was new that year), and "Defender", (the boat owned by the American syndicate which had beaten the previous British challenger, Lord Dunravens "Valkyrie".) The ride and the run of fairs were sold to John Green and Sons in 1925.

(Right) Mitchell's Steam Yachts at Burnley Fair in 1906.

The Steam Yachts when in the ownership of John Green and Sons.

76

Bennie Mitchell's Cocks and Ostriches on a typical Lancashire fairground, probably Bolton. It is possible to see the curved top of the firebox of the centre engine in the middle of the ride, with the circular ends of the twin cylinders above.

1901 No.2 Platform Galloper.

The fist noted appearance of Bennie Mitchell's Cocks is at Oldham Wakes 1901, where it was open alongside the No.1 Platform Ostriches, and the Steam Yachts. It was a second hand machine, but the previous owner is not known. A few years after Bennie's death the ride was advertised for sale by William Mitchell as a *"40 foot Savage built Cocks and Ostriches"* ride . This was a three abreast machine and smaller than the other Platform Galloper. It was sold to Linseys of South Wales.

Platform Galloper sections packed up and ready for the road. Each section carried three mounts, and travelled on the road on the same wheels that ran on the track of the ride when it was built up. The galloping mechanism was disengaged when travelling.

1905 Motor Car Switchback.

This was a rebuild of the No.2 Switchback Galloper with a brand new bottom and a set of eight Motor Cars. Motor cars were introduced on Switchbacks that year, the first set being delivered by Savages on a new machine for Jacob Studt of South Wales. The second set were fitted to Hanna Waddington's ride which previously had Gondola cars. Mitchell's had the third set to be built, and were the first in Lancashire. The ride travelled until 1912, when parts were used in the construction of the new Scenic Railway. On 10th February 1912 William Mitchell Jnr. was advertising: *"For sale, remains of Switchback, and Switchback Horses".* In April 1914 a more detailed list of items was advertised for sale comprising: *6 h.p. Savage centre engine with chimney and pulling frame, a full set of spindle handrails, carved boards for the pulling frame, and all the rounding boards, cornices and droppers.* These were sold to George Wilmot of Glasgow, and fitted into another machine bottom, with motor cars.

Mitchell's Motors with a full load of children

George Wilmot's steam driven Motor Car Switchback at the Kelvin Hall in Glasgow. This machine was constructed using the centre drive unit and pulling frame from Mitchell's Switchback. The ride would normally have a standing top and canvas cover, which have not been fitted as it is operating indoors. The very elaborately carved and decorated boards on the pulling frame, and the ceilings beneath them were specially built for Mitchells. Only one other British machine is known to have been fitted with them (Wallis's), but they were considered a standard fitting on Switchbacks in France and Germany.

A Savage built Razzle Dazzle under test at the Kings Lynn works of the firm in 1906. Mitchells ordered a machine of this type in that year, but later cancelled the order and the ride was completed for Midlands showman Pat Collins.

1906 Razzle Dazzle

In the years after William Mitchell purchased the Razzle Dazzle from Parkers of Bury the design of ride had been improved by several inventors. Howcrofts of West Hartlepool began building two dip steam driven machines in 1905, and the following year Savages of Kings Lynn began to build a ride which had a cycle of eight dips. William Mitchell placed an order for a ride from Savages, which appears on works drawings as order No.3741. At the same time John Collins of Liverpool ordered an identical machine. It was probably this, plus the fact that Edmund Holland, T.Harrison and Relph & Pedley had also taken delivery of Howcroft Razzle Dazzles, that made Mitchells decide to cancel the order. On later drawings the order number was transferred to Pat Collins, who took delivery of the completed machine which was started for Mitchells.

1910 Joy Wheel.

In 1910 the Joy Wheel was introduced to Britain and began to be produced in great numbers. Savages of Kings Lynn built several of these rides, but after many years of loyalty to the Kings Lynn firm Mitchells chose to have their new ride built by Savages main rival, Orton and Spooner of Burton on Trent.

The ride was travelled by Thomas Mitchell and must have been almost new when it made its only appearance at Hull Fair as there is no decoration on the ride, just paper posters. It was later fitted with an entrance surrounded by carved work, and the shutters and rounding boards handsomely decorated and lettered. It was still being travelled in 1912 when the Scenic Railway was delivered, but ceased to travel at some time after that.

Lettered panel from Mitchell's Joy Wheel.

1914-15 Four Abreast Gallopers

This was a Savage built ride which was new to Harry Wallis of Liverpool in 1895. It was fitted with centre engine number 628, and organ engine 625. It was sold to Bennie Mitchell in 1914-15 and probably took the place of his platform galloper at most fairs. Following Bennie's untimely death the ride was operated by his widow and two young sons. At some time during Mitchell's ownership it was fitted with a new set of rounding boards. It became the sole machine of Mitchells to travel after the Yachts were sold and the Scenic was packed up. Attempts were made to sell it in the early 1930's, but at that time faster modern machines had made Gallopers almost worthless, and the ride was broken up for parts. The rounding boards were cut down and used on John Collins' three abreast, and the organ was sold to Silcock Bros. to use in their Waltzer. The rounding boards outlived the Collins machine and were fitted to Edmund Holland's three abreast in the 1940's. They remained in use on this third machine until the late 1950's.

1912 Scenic Railway

Electrically driven Scenic Railways had been introduced in 1910. In 1912 Mitchells placed an order with Orton and Spooner of Burton On Trent to rebuild their Motor Switchback and convert it to electric drive. This was the first ride of any kind to be fitted with a proper extension front, previous machines had small porches over the front steps, but on Mitchell's the rounding boards swept gracefully out to the large front boards. A large staff was required for the ride as can be seen from an advert for staff in the Worlds Fair of May 1912:

Wanted

*12 good men, Best wages given
for Mitchell's new Scenic Railway
also two first-class traction engine drivers
Mitchell's Roundabout Works, Heywood*

The rear of the machine was reported to be fitted with striking willow pattern scenery and a waterfall. The ride remained open during the winter

Preston Whit Fair 1930 showing Mitchell's four abreast with the new rounding boards; W.H.Jennings Chairoplanes; and at the extreme left are John Green and Sons' (ex Mitchell's) Steam Yachts.

William Mitchell's Scenic Railway showing the elaborate scenery around the organ.

of 1912 at Spekeland Road in Liverpool, accompanied by William Mitchell's Racing Cockerels and Steam Yachts.

At the end of the Great War a completely new bottom was fitted to the machine by Orton and Spooners, but despite this expense the ride was packed away in the late 1920's.

Another advert in the Worlds Fair details the sale of the ride in 1930:

For Sale:
One spider Scenic Railway bottom, complete with centre truck, gantry, sleepers, trams, carved handrails, gates, run-ups, steps back and front, standing top, rounding boards, cornice, droppers, and pillars. All made by Orton & Spooner. Extension to front steps, good as new, only used one season. Apply William Mitchell Snr. 64 Egerton Street, Heywood, Lancs.

The ride was sold to Michael Albert Collins and the bottom of the machine was used in his Savage Scenic. Other parts of the ride were presumably used as spares on Collins Bros. two Scenic Railways.

The bottom and handrails of Mitchell's scenic fitted to Michael Albert Collins Dragons

1931 Orton & Spooner Noah's Ark

When the Scenic Railway went off the road in the late 1920's William Mitchell Jnr. and his son Jack had no adult machines travelling. In 1930 Noah's Arks were introduced to the country from Germany, and were a great success. Mitchell's ordered a new machine from Orton and Spooner, which was delivered early in 1931.

It was a standard 42 ft. 18 platform machine with a two bay extension front. In 1933 Ortons fitted a a better set of rounding boards which were unique on a Noah's Ark type ride being framed, with the centre panel canvassed, and decorated with top quality cartoon scenes. The ride was also fitted with carved false pillars on all the uprights, some of which are reputed to have come from Davies' Scenic Dolphins.

When the Four Abreast came off the road at the end of 1932 the Ark took over some of the positions that it had travelled. In 1936 a set of Motorbikes was fitted in place of the outside row of animals, and in 1937 the extension front was enlarged to four sections and decorated with motor racing scenes. In 1958 the flights and inside scenery were replaced with a revolving ceiling. this revolved in the opposite direction to the platforms and gave the illusion of increased speed to the riders when they looked up. At the same time the extension front was modified and fitted flush with the uprights, and the ride was fitted with a canopy over the front steps.

In 1959 the Scottish firm of Maxwells delivered a set of nine Waltzer cars. From this time the ride could be operated either as an Ark or as a Waltzer. The ride had been travelled by Jack Mitchell after his father's death, but in 1965 he made his cousin Billy (Bennie's son) a partner. Jack died in 1966, just before the ride was taken in part exchange by Maxwells for a new Speedway ride.

The Orton machine was sold to Stanley Codona and travelled Scotland until 1980 when it was sold to Freddie Dean in the South of England. It travelled exclusively as a Waltzer until 1996 when it was sold to Steve Shannon of Brighton, and the following year it was sold to Dave Jones. The ride was again sold as recently as 2002, and is believed to be stored in Lincolnshire.

Preston Whit Fair 1934. This is taken from the same position as the photograph on page 80. It shows Mitchell's Ark on the Four-Abreast position. Jack Whyatt's Yachts in place of green Bros. machine, and Hibble & Mellor's Mont Blanc, which was travelled that season by Green Bros., on their Caterpillar position. Only Jennings Chairoplanes remain in the same position.

Jack Mitchell's Speedway Ark at Bolton in 1941 fitted with the enlarged extension front and the pillars with carved capitals which are believed to have come from William Davies' Dolphin Scenic Railway.

The same ride at Middleton on 19th June 1959, operating as a Waltzer with the extension front cut down and fitted flush to the uprights. The elaborate rounding boards with the recessed panels were unique.

The last adult riding machine to bear the name of the Lancashire Mitchells was this Maxwell built Speedway ride photographed in a later ownership in Lancashire but still bearing Mitchell's name. (Michael Smith).

1966 Maxwell Speedway

This ride was delivered to Burnley Wakes Fair in July 1966 six months after Jack Mitchell's death. It was travelled by Billy Mitchell and his son-in-law Jeff Jeffries. It soon passed into the ownership of Jeff and Dorothy, and from 1976 it travelled under the partnership of Silcock and Jeffries. The following year it became the sole property of H.Silcock, and in 1979 passed to Arthur Silcock. For eight years it travelled alongside Silcocks very similar 1972 Speedway/Waltzer conversion, the two machines opening alongside each other at many places. For one season in 1987 it travelled as

Glynn de Koning's, but the following year was back in the ownership of Arthur Silcock. At this time the bold experiment of fitting swinging cars to the platform was attempted, but was not a great success, and the ride continued to travel as a Speedway until 1990 when it was sold to Tommy McIntyre of Scotland who travelled the ride as a Waltzer, replacing his previous Waltzer which was a conversion of one of the first Arks to come into the country in 1930. In 1993 the ride came back to England when it was sold to Raynor Fletcher of Cumbria, and it reverted back to a Speedway and travelled alongside his much older Waltzer ride. At present the ride remains in his ownership.

ESTABLISHED WHEN
GEORGE IV WAS KING.

PERMANENT ADDRESS :—
6 Manchester Street, HEYWOOD,
Nr. MANCHESTER.

MEMO. FROM   19

WM. MITCHELL & SON,
AMUSEMENT CATERERS.

To ,,...

....

A letterhead used by Mitchells in the 1930's which proclaims the founding of the firm to date from the 1820's when George IV was King.

MITCHELLS' ENGINES

It is well recorded that William Mitchell at one time used dogs to transport his wares to Lancashire fairgrounds. This was not uncommon, large dogs were specially bred in Holland and Belgium for working with barges, and they were equally at home pulling a dog cart. The practice became illegal in Britain, and at that time a change to horses would have been made. Horse teams were quite capable of transporting large rides around as the rides broke down into convenient small parts, and were packed into trucks around 12 ft. long which could be managed by one or two horses on the flat. With the coming of steam power to drive the rides the heaviest piece of equipment was the centre truck which carried the steam engine, and even these were transported by teams of horses. On longer journeys the loads would be taken to a railway goods yard and loaded onto flat carriage trucks, and then delivered by horses from the rail destination to the fairground.

McLaren Traction Centre No.95

In 1880 McLarens of Leeds invented the traction centre engine. This was a road engine which would transport the loads of the ride, and once on the fairground it was used as the centre truck of the ride which was built up around it, and it was used to drive the ride.

William Mitchell was one of the first showmen to use a traction centre engine in his 1881 Sea on Land, This was a 6 h.p. single cylinder McLaren engine number 95. It was eventually converted to a standard road engine and was sold out of the business to W.Tanfield of Beverly in East Yorkshire.

McLaren Traction Centre No.100

The following year a second Sea on Land was bought from Hill & Sons of Bristol. This was fitted with McLaren number 100, a 6 h.p. single cylinder of the same batch as Mitchell's original engine.

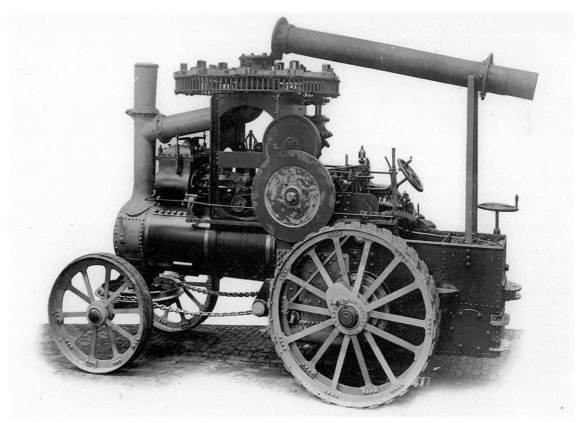

Photographs of McLaren traction centre engines are almost non existent, however the excellent Fowler works photo of John Cramptons Traction Centre from his Gallopers shows an engine similar in most respects to the McLaren engines which were owned by Mitchells .

William Codona's 6 h.p. McLaren traction engine number 91 on a fairground in Scotland. This engine was only four numbers away from Mitchell's first traction centre, and the basic engine would have been almost identical .As with Mitchell's later McLaren road engine this was used for haulage, and to generate electricity on the fairgrounds when they were open. Later showmen's engines were fitted with a bracket in front of the smokebox to carry the dynamo, but earlier engines without this feature were frequently set in line with a dynamo mounted on a truck. The open frame dynamo on the truck can be clearly seen in the above photograph.

McLaren traction engine No.169

This engine was new In 1883 to a contractor from Oldham named Jackson Clough. It was a 6 h.p. single cylinder and as such was very similar to the two Mitchell traction centres. Clough was the son of a farmer at Chadderton near Oldham, and in his capacity as contractor it is quite possible that the engine was used to move fairground equipment for showmen. In 1888 the engine was sold to William Mitchell for use with his rides. It was later sold to L.Flint of County Meath in Ireland.

McLaren traction engine No.523

This was supplied new to William Mitchell in November 1894. It was an 8 h.p. compound cylinder engine, and must have been a great improvement on the 6 h.p. single cylinder traction centres. It is recorded as having been fitted with Boulton Woodblock wheels. This was a patented idea of covering the steel outer running rim of the wheel in wood blocks as an attempt to give better adhesion. In Lancashire and Yorkshire particularly many miles of highway were paved with stone setts, and on a wet day on a gradient an engine with a heavy load could easily start to skid when it was

running on metal wheels. It is recorded as having been named *Lancashire Lass,* but was known to the family as *Shall I Do It.* It was a plain road engine without a canopy or a dynamo bracket and on the fairgrounds it had to be lined up with a dynamo fitted to a truck to generate electricity. It had a long working life of around thirty years with Mitchells, latterly used by Thomas Mitchell accompanying the Steam Yachts. When road vehicle registration was introduced it was registered as TB3705. It is believed to have been sold to and used by W.H.Jennings.

Garrett Road Locomotive No.27360

The firm of Garret of Leiston, Suffolk, achieved some popularity with their smaller steam tractors amongst showmen, but this engine was unusual on the fairgrounds in being a 7 h.p. compound engine. It was new to R.H.Hayne and Co. of Ardwick, Manchester in 1909, and was sold about 1912 to William Mitchell at the time when they bought the Scenic Railway. It recieved road registration number CK3407. After only a couple of years it was sold to showman J.Dewhurst of Preston and worked with his three abreast gallopers.

Foster Road Locomotive No.12940

This engine was new to Mitchells on 13th August 1912, specifically to power the new Orton & Spooner Scenic Railway. Fosters had developed the 65 b.hp. engines for working with rides of this type, and although three had already been delivered, this engine, which was named *Lancashire Lad*, was the first to be delivered with the rear facing extension to the dynamo bracket for carrying a second auxiliary dynamo between the cylinders and the chimney. The engine received the road registration number TB3704. After a short time it was fitted with a Thompson and Walton pillar crane at the rear, which was used for lifting the heavy scenic cars on and off the track of the ride, utilising the wire rope winch which was a standard feature on showman's engines. The engine worked with the ride until it stopped travelling in the late 1920's, and after only a short break it was put to work with Mitchell's new Noah's Ark. It travelled with this ride until August 1945 when it was laid up at Radcliffe. It was later cut up at Green Street, Radcliffe, but the main dynamo was retained for use on a diesel powered lighting set.

Foster Road Locomotive No.3664

This was an 8h.p. SRL class of showman's engine which was supplied new to Harry Wallis of Seaforth to accompany his Four Abreast Gallopers. It was named *Her Majesty*, and carried the road registration number TB2966. In 1914-15 it was sold with the ride to Bennie Mitchell. When Bennie died in 1919 the ride and engine were travelled by his two sons. In the early 1930's the engine worked for a short time with William Mitchell's Noah's Ark, but was sold after 1932 to Arthur Bates of Rhode Heath. It originally travelled with his Over the Tops ride, a heavy build up type of Swinging Gyms. Bates and Mitchell's runs of fairs overlapped quite considerably and the engine was often to be found with its old stable mate *Lancashire Lad* on many fairgrounds.

Foden Road Locomotive No.2106

This 6 h.p. compound engine named *Dreadnought* was new in 1910 to Simons and Greatorex of Nantwich to accompany their three abreast Gallopers. Fodens of Sandbach did not build many engines specifically for showmen and

"Lancashire Lad" at Heywood in 1940. By this time the engine had already been in constant use with Mitchells for twenty eight years, and it was to continue working with the Noah's Ark ride for a further five years.

Harry Wallis's Foster showman's engine "Her Majesty" which was sold to Bennie Mitchell in 1914-15.

Garrett Showman's engine number 27360. This engine was new in 1909 to a haulage contractor, but was bought by William Mitchell when it was only three years old. It was converted to a showman's engine with a dynamo bracket and full length cab. As a 7 h.p. engine of this make it was very much a rarity on the fairgrounds. It was sold to James Dewhurst of Preston and travelled with his three abreast Gallopers until the late 1940's. (J.Palmer).

Foster showman's engine "Irene" which was purchased by William Mitchell in 1922 when it was three years old. It was used with W.H.Jennings Chairoplanes ride until 1937 when it was sold to the Cheetham family based at Pickmere Lake.

this was their last example. Following the death of Thomas Mitchell in 1919 one of the first things his widow Rachael did was to get rid of the old McLaren traction engine *Shall I Do It*, and replace it with this Foden. During Mitchell's ownership it worked with their Steam Yachts, and received the Bolton road registration number BN4916. In 1925 it was sold to Henry O'Brien in Scotland, and worked during the 1930's with a Jack and Jill ride. In 1939 it was sold out of showland to R.Hamilton of Hurlford.

Foster Road Locomotive No.14386

This was a 7 h.p. SRL class of showman's engine named *Irene*, supplied new to James Traynor of Preston. It carried the road registration number CK3408. In 1922 it was sold to William Mitchell, and by 1928 it was travelling with his son-in-law W.H. Jennings Chairoplanes. In 1937 it was sold to the Cheshire Amusement Company, also known as the Pickmere Boat Company, to travel a Noah's Ark ride.

Two photographs taken at Nelson Fair in 1948. The four wheel Armstrong Saurer lorry was bought from Corrigans of Yorkshire in 1945 to replace the engine "Lancashire Lad". The box truck was one of two used to transport the Noah's Ark ride.

Mack tractor HTC 830 "Lancashire Lad" which replaced the Armstrong Saurer, photographed by Jack Mitchell at Nelson Fair 1949. As well as carrying the generating sets the tractor is fitted with a rear mounted crane, probably for lifting the centre truck when removing or fitting the axle and wheels.

Also taken at Nelson by Jack Mitchell is a second Mack tractor "Lancashire Lass" which travelled with the Ark, registered KTF268 . There is a large ballast stone over the back wheels. The lattice tower is part of the crane for lifting the platforms. Jack Mitchell took up photography as a hobby and these two photographs were taken with his Leica. Jack developed and printed his own photographs.

WANTED KNOWN
to all
Showmen, Roundabout Proprietors,
Stallholders and others, that
I am now booking Spaces for my

SUMMER RUN,

at the following places :
HOLLINWOOD WAKES,
July 24th to 28th;
LEES WAKES,
July 31 to August 2;
ACCRINGTON AUGUST FAIR,
commencing August 6th to 11th.
HEYWOOD WAKES,
August to 7 to 11;
ROCHDALE WAKES,
August 14 to 24;;
LITTLE HULTON POOR
DICK'S WAKES,
September 11 to 15.
and other places right up to the end
of the season.
No Swinging Balls or Cue Billiards
allowed.
Apply to
MITCHELL & SONS,
53, Hindhill Street, Heywood,
or en route

(Above Left) Jack Mitchell and his sister Janie. Jack was in charge of the Orton and Spooner Noah's Ark from it being new . He had part control of the business from 1931 and ran it after his father's death in 1946. Jack handed the business over to his cousin Billy (Bennie's son), shortly before his death in 1966.
(Above Right) A 1915 advert from the showmen's newspaper "The Worlds Fair" for spaces to let on the Summer Run run of fairs controlled by Mitchells.

Mitchell's Ark with the original smaller two bay front at Bolton in 1934. To the right are Crick's Mono Rail, Mitchell's Mono Rail and M.A.Collins Waltzer.

Typewriting Championships

International Competitions taken part in by Eleanor Mitchell

1922 Paris

Tied with the previous years champion in speed contest, but was awarded second prize.

1923 Paris

Second in the speed contest. Won Repetee phrase contest.

1924 Paris

First in speed contest. Won two awards.

1925 Paris

November. First in speed contest.

December. First in speed contest, Second copying from previously unseen manuscript.

1926

June. Paris

July. Auxerre

July. Rome. Won championship.

December. Paris. First in speed contest.

1927 Paris

May.

December. First in speed contest

1928 Paris

October. First in speed contest. Awarded Challenge Cup.

1929 Versailles.

November. First in speed contest.

1930 Paris.

November. First in speed contest. 20% faster than nearest opponent.

Mitchell Family Tree

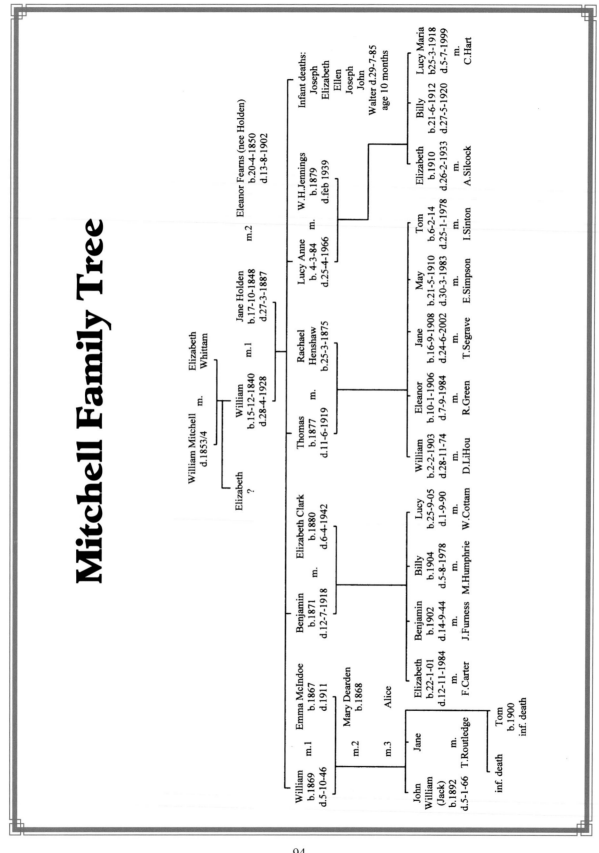

Henshaw Family Tree

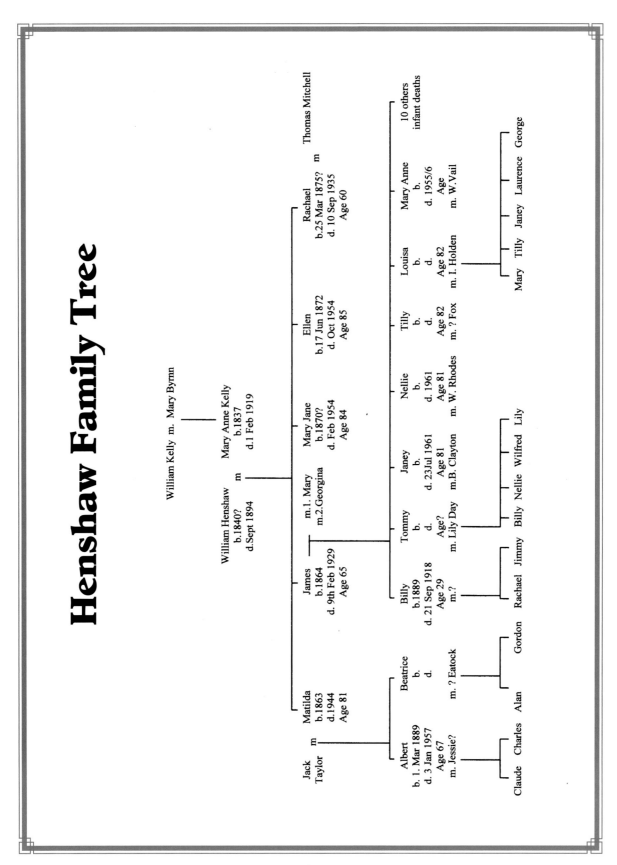

William Kelly m. Mary Byrnn

Mary Anne Kelly
b.1837
d.1 Feb 1919

William Henshaw   m
b.1840?
d.Sept 1894

m.1. Mary
m.2.Georgina

James
b.1864
d. 9th Feb 1929
Age 65

Matilda
b.1863
d.1944
Age 81

Jack
Taylor   m

Rachael
b.25 Mar 1875?
d. 10 Sep 1935
Age 60

Thomas Mitchell   m

Ellen
b.17 Jun 1872
d. Oct 1954
Age 85

Mary Jane
b.1870?
d. Feb 1954
Age 84

10 others
infant deaths

Mary Anne
b.
d. 1955/6
Age
m. W.Vail

Louisa
b.
d.
Age 82
m. I. Holden

Tilly
b.
d.
Age 82
m. ? Fox

Nellie
b.
d. 1961
Age 81
m. W. Rhodes

Janey
b.
d. 23Jul 1961
Age 81
m.B. Clayton

Tommy
b.
d.
Age?
m. Lily Day

Billy
b.1889
d. 21 Sep 1918
Age 29
m.?

Beatrice
b.
d.
m. ? Eatock

Albert
b. 1. Mar 1889
d. 3 Jan 1957
Age 67
m. Jessie?

Mary Tilly Janey Laurence George

Lily

Billy Nellie Wilfred

Rachael Jimmy

Gordon

Claude Charles Alan

95

Sketch of Grandad Mitchell which appeared in the
"Worlds Fair" in 1926.
Drawn by Thomas C Green, Eleanor's Brother-in-Law.